EMMA MAXWELL

Estate Planning Made Easy

Contents

Introduction   vi

Chapter 1   1

  Understanding the Basics of Estate Planning   1

    1.1 What is Estate Planning? Demystifying the Basics 1

    1.2 Trusts vs. Wills: Making the Right Choice for You 3

    1.3 Breaking Down the Probate Process   5

    1.4 The Role of Executors and Trustees: Choosing Wisely 6

    1.5 Legal Jargon Simplified: Key Terms You Need to Know 8

    1.6 The Importance of Starting Early: Securing Your Legacy 9

Chapter 2   12

  Tailoring Your Estate Plan to Fit Your Needs   12

    2.1 Estate Planning for Blended and Non-Traditional Families 12

    2.2 Guardianship for Minor Children: Ensuring Their Future 14

    2.3 High-Net-Worth Estate Strategies: Protecting Large Estates 16

    2.4 Business Succession Planning: Ensuring Smooth Transitions 18

    2.5 Equitable Asset Distribution: Balancing Family Dynamics 19

    2.6 Navigating Unique Cultural and Regional Considerations 21

Chapter 3   24

  Avoiding Common Pitfalls and Mistakes   24

    3.1 Avoiding Probate: Strategies and Benefits   26

    3.2 Common Mistakes in Will Creation and How to Avoid Them 28

    3.3 Understanding Tax Implications and Strategies   29

    3.4 Choosing the Right Legal and Financial Advisors   31

3.5 The Perils of Procrastination: Why Estate Planning
Can't Wait   33

Chapter 4   35

  Organizing and Documenting Your Assets   35

    4.1 Essential Documents for Estate Planning 37

    4.2 Using Technology to Manage and Protect Your Estate 38

    4.3 Documenting Wishes: Healthcare Directives and More 40

    4.4 Digital Assets: Protecting Your Online Presence 41

    4.5 Long-Term Storage Solutions: Keeping Your Documents Secure 43

Chapter 5   46

  Engaging Professional Help Wisely   46

    5.1 When to Consult a Lawyer: Knowing Your Limits 46

    5.2 Interviewing Lawyers: Asking the Right Questions 48

    5.3 Understanding the Cost of Professional Services 50

    5.4 Collaborating with Financial Advisors for Estate Planning 51

    5.5 The Role of Executors: Selecting and Guiding Them 53

    5.6 Planning for Incapacity: Powers of Attorney and More 54

    5.7 Building a Reliable Support Team: Your Estate
Planning Allies   56

Chapter 6   59

  Special Considerations and Advanced Strategies   59

    6.1 Charitable Giving and Estate Planning: Creating a Legacy 59

    6.2 Leveraging Tax Havens: Legal Considerations 61

    6.3 Navigating International Estates: Cross-Border Planning 63

    6.4 Using Life Insurance in Estate Planning 64

    6.5 Asset Protection Trusts: Shielding Your Wealth 66

Chapter 7   69

  Real-Life Examples and Case Studies   69

    7.1 Case Study: Retirees Finalizing Their Legacies 71

    7.2 Case Study: High-Net-Worth Individuals Preserving Wealth 72

    7.3 Case Study: Parents Securing Their Children's Futures 74

7.4 Case Study: Blended Families Achieving Equitable Distribution   76

7.5 Lessons Learned from Common Mistakes in Estate Planning   77

Chapter 8   80

Maintaining and Updating Your Estate Plan   80

8.1 Life Changes and Estate Planning: When to Update   80

8.2 Conducting an Annual Estate Plan Review   82

8.3 Keeping Up with Legal Changes: Staying Informed   84

8.4 Communicating Your Plan to Family Members   85

8.5 Digital Tools and Resources for Ongoing Management   87

8.6 Creating a Legacy Beyond Financial Planning   88

Conclusion   91

References   94

Also by Emma Maxwell   97

Introduction

Have you ever wondered what would happen to your loved ones if something unexpected happened to you? It's a sobering thought, but one that far too many people put off addressing until it's too late. The truth is, estate planning isn't just for the wealthy or the elderly – it's a crucial step that everyone should take to protect their assets and ensure their final wishes are carried out.

As a Certified Public Accountant (CPA), I've seen firsthand the confusion and stress that can arise when families are left to navigate the complex world of estate planning without proper guidance. That's why I've made it my mission to demystify this process and make it accessible to everyone, regardless of their financial situation or family structure.

In this book, "Estate Planning Made Easy: Step-by-Step Guide to Protect your Assets, Minimize Estate Taxes, and Ease the Financial Burden for your Family," I'll walk you through the essential components of a comprehensive estate plan, from creating a will to establishing healthcare directives. You'll learn how to tailor your plan to your unique circumstances, regardless of your age, gender or marital status.

But this isn't just another dry, technical manual. I believe that estate planning doesn't have to be intimidating or overwhelming. By breaking down complex concepts into simple, actionable steps, I'll show you how to take control of your legacy and provide peace of mind for yourself and your loved ones.

Throughout the book, you'll find real-world case studies that illustrate how proper estate planning can make a profound difference in people's lives. You'll also discover how to avoid common pitfalls and misconceptions that can derail even the best-laid plans.

Whether you're starting from scratch or looking to update an existing plan, this book will be your go-to resource. I've designed it to be a comprehensive guide that covers all the bases, from the basics of asset distribution to more complex topics like trusts and tax implications.

But perhaps most importantly, I want to empower you to take action. Estate planning isn't something you can afford to put off until tomorrow. By taking the first step today, you'll be giving your family an invaluable gift – the security and peace of mind that comes from knowing you've planned for every eventuality.

As someone who's passionate about helping people navigate life's financial challenges, I'm excited to share my expertise with you. With over thirty years of experience as a CPA, I've guided countless individuals and families to create their estate plans that reflect their values and priorities. I'm not an estate lawyer, but I am knowledgeable enough to give guidance to help put you in touch with the best professionals you'll need.

So, what will you gain from this book? Here are the key takeaways:

- The difference between wills and trusts
- How to avoid probate and maintain your family's privacy
- Tax strategies to minimize estate taxes
- How to choose the best executors and trustees including guardianship
- How to communicate to your beneficiaries your estate plan
- Setting up powers of attorney and healthcare directives
- How to hire the best professionals to help you
- Best ways to organize and document your estate plan

Like all my other books, at the end of each chapter there are practical, actionable steps that you can take to improve where you're at with your estate plan. You'll find that these principles are not just theory, they're real solutions that can make a difference in your life.

So whether you're a busy parent trying to safeguard your children's future, a retiree looking to ensure a smooth transition of assets, or a business owner seeking to protect your hard-earned legacy, this book is for you. Together, we'll cut through the jargon and confusion to create a clear, concise plan that works for your unique situation.

Throughout this book, you'll learn how to assess your current estate plan. You'll explore what you need to do to get prepared and in the best position for you and your family. This book is structured logically, starting with the basics and moving on to the more advanced topics. Here's a brief overview of the chapters:

1. Understanding the Basics of Estate Planning
2. Tailoring Your Estate Plan to Fit Your Needs
3. Avoiding Common Pitfalls and Mistakes
4. Organizing and Documenting Your Assets
5. Engaging Professional Help Wisely
6. Special Considerations and Advanced Strategies
7. Real-Life Examples and Case Studies
8. Maintaining and Updating Your Estate Plan

Are you ready to take control of your legacy? Let's get started on this journey together – one step at a time. Turn the page, and let's begin building an estate plan that will give you and your loved ones the peace of mind you deserve.

Chapter 1

Understanding the Basics of Estate Planning

When was the last time you took a moment to really think about your future and the legacy you wish to leave behind? It's a question that often lingers in the back of our minds, yet many of us delay confronting it until circumstances force our hand. Estate planning, a term that might sound daunting or reserved for the affluent, is, in fact, a vital process for everyone. Whether you're gearing up for retirement, managing a thriving business, or raising a young family, having a plan in place is crucial. It ensures that your wishes are honored, your family is cared for, and your assets are distributed as you intend. So, what exactly is estate planning, and why is it so indispensable?

1.1 What is Estate Planning? Demystifying the Basics

At its core, estate planning is the methodical process of preparing for the eventual distribution and management of your assets upon your incapacitation or passing. This involves creating a comprehensive plan that details how your possessions, both tangible and intangible, will be handled. Importantly, estate planning isn't just about drafting a will or setting up a trust. It encompasses a range of legal instruments and directives that safeguard your interests and those of your loved ones. Wills, trusts, and powers of attorney are fundamental components of this process, each serving a distinct purpose. A will outlines your wishes regarding asset allocation and guardianship for minor children, while a trust facilitates the management of your assets during your lifetime and beyond. Powers of attorney ensure that someone you trust can make decisions on your behalf if you're unable to do so.

The necessity of estate planning transcends age and wealth. It's not solely the purview of the elderly or the affluent. Regardless of your asset size, having a plan in place is crucial. It protects not only your financial legacy but also your family's future. Consider, for instance, the misconception that estate planning is reserved for the wealthy. This myth often deters individuals from taking steps to secure their assets. Yet, the reality is that estate planning is relevant to anyone who wishes to have a say in how their assets are managed and distributed when they pass. It's about taking control and ensuring that your legacy aligns with your values and intentions.

The goals of estate planning are manifold but can be distilled into three primary objectives: asset protection, minimizing taxes, and ensuring family security. Asset protection involves shielding your wealth from unnecessary depletion due to creditors or legal challenges. By establishing trusts or utilizing other legal strategies, you can maintain control over your assets, ensuring they are used according to your wishes. Minimizing taxes is another critical aspect. Through careful planning, you can reduce the tax burden on your estate, preserving more of your wealth for your heirs. This involves understanding the implications of estate and gift taxes and employing strategies to mitigate their impact. Finally, ensuring family security is paramount. With a well-crafted estate plan, you provide for your loved ones, safeguarding their financial future and minimizing potential disputes.

Common misconceptions about estate planning abound. Many people believe it's only necessary for the elderly or those with vast fortunes. However, estate planning is vital for anyone who wishes to dictate how their assets are distributed. Another prevalent myth is that without significant assets, a plan is unnecessary. This couldn't be further from the truth. Estate planning is about more than wealth; it's about intention and foresight. It's about ensuring that your wishes are carried out and that your loved ones are protected.

The benefits of estate planning extend beyond asset distribution. It offers peace of mind, knowing that your family's future is secure and your wishes are documented. It prevents family disputes by providing clear instructions, reducing the likelihood of misunderstandings. Moreover, it streamlines the inheritance process, ensuring a smooth transition of assets. This is particularly crucial for blended or non-traditional families, where dynamics can be complex.

Estate planning is a thoughtful process that reflects your values, priorities, and love for those you cherish. Through it, you create a road map for the future, one that provides clarity and security. As we explore this topic further, you'll discover the tools and strategies needed to craft a plan that suits your unique circumstances. Whether you're a middle-aged parent, a retiree, or a business owner, the journey to understanding estate planning is one of empowerment and foresight.

1.2 Trusts vs. Wills: Making the Right Choice for You

Navigating the realm of estate planning often begins with a fundamental question: should you opt for a trust or a will? Each tool serves a distinct purpose, tailored to different needs and situations. A will is a legal document that outlines how you want your assets distributed after your death. It allows you to appoint guardians for minor children and specify your wishes in a straightforward manner. Trusts, on the other hand, are legal arrangements where a trustee holds and manages assets on behalf of beneficiaries. One of the most significant advantages of a trust is its ability to bypass the probate process, offering a layer of privacy and speed in asset distribution that wills cannot. Probate, the court-supervised process of validating a will, can be lengthy and public, making trusts an attractive option for those who value discretion and efficiency.

Deciding whether to use a trust or a will often depends on your specific circumstances and goals. For many, a simple will is suffice, especially when dealing with smaller estates or straightforward asset distribution. Wills are generally easier and less expensive to set up, making them an accessible option for those with uncomplicated financial situations. However, there are instances when a trust may be more appropriate. If you have significant assets, wish to avoid probate, or have beneficiaries who may not be financially responsible, a trust can offer you more control over how and when your assets are distributed. A revocable living trust, for example, allows you to manage your assets during your lifetime and provides flexibility, as you can alter the trust as your situation changes. This flexibility makes it a popular choice for those with evolving needs or complex family dynamics.

The benefits of trusts and wills extend beyond their basic functions. Trusts provide privacy, as they do not go through the public probate process. This can be particularly beneficial for high-net-worth individuals or those who prefer to keep their financial matters confidential. Additionally, trusts can be structured to offer protection from creditors, further safeguarding your estate. Wills, on the other hand, are known for their simplicity and cost-effectiveness. They are an effective way to communicate your wishes clearly, ensuring that your assets are distributed according to your intentions. The cost of setting up a will is typically lower than that of a trust, making it a practical choice for many.

When considering estate planning, common questions often arise. One frequent inquiry is whether you can have both a trust and a will. The answer is yes; they can complement each other effectively. A "pour-over" will, for instance, can work alongside a trust, ensuring any assets not included in the trust are still managed according to your wishes. Another question is how each tool affects taxes and probate. While trusts generally help avoid probate, they do not automatically confer tax benefits unless structured specifically for that purpose. Wills are subject to probate, which can involve additional time and expenses. However, both instruments can be crafted with tax efficiency in mind, depending on your estate planning goals.

Understanding the roles and advantages of trusts and wills allows you to make informed decisions about your estate plan. Whether you choose a will, a trust, or a combination of both, the key is to tailor your plan to your unique circumstances. This ensures that your assets are managed and distributed in a way that aligns with your values and fulfills your objectives. As you contemplate these options, consider your priorities, the complexity of your estate, and the level of control you wish to maintain over your legacy.

1.3 Breaking Down the Probate Process

The probate process can seem like a mysterious and daunting legal hurdle, but understanding its steps can demystify it significantly. Probate begins with the initial filing and validation of the deceased's will. This step is crucial, as the court must confirm the will's authenticity before any further action is taken. Once validated, an executor—appointed by the will or the court—takes charge of the estate. The next step involves a comprehensive inventory of the deceased's assets. This includes both tangible assets like real estate and vehicles, as well as intangible ones such as stocks and insurance policies. An appraisal may be necessary to determine their value accurately, ensuring a clear picture of the estate's worth. With the inventory complete, the executor moves to settle any debts or obligations. This means notifying creditors and paying off any outstanding liabilities, from mortgages to unpaid taxes. Only after these debts are cleared can the executor proceed to distribute the remaining assets to the designated beneficiaries.

Probate serves a vital function by providing legal oversight and ensuring the deceased's wishes are honored. It can resolve disputes by offering a structured process under judicial supervision. However, this benefit comes with notable drawbacks. The process can be time-consuming, often taking months or even years to conclude, depending on the estate's complexity. This delay can cause financial strain for beneficiaries who might depend on timely access to their inheritance. Additionally, probate can be costly, with legal fees and court costs eating into the estate's value. Another disadvantage is the lack of privacy, as probate proceedings are public records. This means anyone can access details about the estate's assets and the beneficiaries, which some families may find intrusive.

Many people seek to avoid probate due to these drawbacks. One effective strategy is setting up a living trust, which allows assets to bypass probate entirely. By transferring ownership of assets to the trust during their lifetime, individuals can ensure a smoother transition upon their death. Designating beneficiaries on financial accounts, such as retirement funds and life insurance policies, is another way to simplify the inheritance process. These assets can transfer directly to the beneficiaries without the need for probate, providing them with quicker access.

Real-life implications of probate can be profound. Consider a family waiting anxiously as the probate process drags on, delaying their access to vital funds needed for daily expenses or education costs. Such delays can lead to frustration and tension among family members. Additionally, the public nature of probate can expose sensitive financial details, causing discomfort or even conflict when family members learn of unexpected bequests or disparities in asset distribution. For instance, a family might face unwanted scrutiny or pressure if the details of a substantial inheritance become public knowledge.

By understanding the probate process, you can make informed decisions about how best to manage your estate. While probate has its place, exploring options to circumvent it can save your family time, money, and stress.

1.4 The Role of Executors and Trustees: Choosing Wisely

In the landscape of estate planning, the roles of executors and trustees are pivotal, yet they serve distinctly different functions. An executor is tasked with the execution of a will, ensuring that the deceased's final wishes are honored, from settling debts to distributing assets. This individual acts as the legal representative in probate court, navigating the complexities of legal requirements and procedural steps. In contrast, a trustee administers the assets within a trust. This role involves managing the trust's assets, making decisions about investments, and disbursing funds to beneficiaries according to the trust's stipulations. Both roles require a level of diligence and integrity, as they carry the weight of executing someone's last wishes.

Selecting the right person for these roles is critical to the smooth implementation of your estate plan. Trustworthiness and reliability are paramount; you want someone with a proven track record of honesty and dependability. Financial acumen is equally important, especially for trustees, who must make prudent financial decisions. This doesn't mean they need to be financial experts, but they should have a basic understanding of financial matters and be willing to seek professional advice when necessary. Consider their ability to communicate effectively and navigate potential family dynamics, as these skills can prevent misunderstandings and conflicts. Reflect on their personal circumstances—are they in a position to take on these responsibilities without undue burden?

The duties of executors and trustees are extensive and varied. Executors are responsible for gathering and inventorying the deceased's assets, notifying creditors, and settling debts. They must also handle tax filings and ensure the distribution of assets aligns with the will. Trustees, meanwhile, must manage the trust assets, which could include real estate, investments, or business interests. They need to balance the interests of various beneficiaries, making decisions that could impact them financially and personally. Both roles require meticulous record-keeping and transparency, as they may need to provide accounts to beneficiaries or the court.

Challenges often arise in these roles, testing the resolve and skills of executors and trustees. Family disagreements are common, especially if beneficiaries feel the estate is not being handled fairly. Executors and trustees must navigate these tensions delicately, ensuring that all actions are justified and transparent. Complex financial decisions can also pose significant challenges. Executors might need to decide which assets to liquidate to pay debts, while trustees may face decisions about investment strategies that could impact the trust's long-term viability. These decisions require careful consideration and, at times, consultation with financial or legal professionals.

In preparing for these roles, it's vital to set clear expectations and provide comprehensive guidance. This means outlining duties in the estate plan, offering insights into the deceased's intentions, and ensuring executors and trustees have access to necessary resources. With the right preparation and support, executors and trustees can fulfill their roles effectively, honoring the legacy and intentions of those who entrusted them with such significant responsibilities.

1.5 Legal Jargon Simplified: Key Terms You Need to Know

Navigating the intricacies of estate planning requires a basic understanding of legal terminology. Without this knowledge, even the simplest discussions can become tangled in confusion. To avoid these pitfalls, it's helpful to familiarize yourself with some essential terms. Probate, for instance, is the legal process through which a deceased person's will is validated and their estate is distributed. Understanding probate is crucial because it affects how and when beneficiaries receive their inheritance. A beneficiary, another critical term, refers to any person or organization entitled to receive a portion of the estate as outlined in a will or trust. Beneficiaries are central to estate planning, as they are the individuals or entities who will ultimately benefit from your assets. Meanwhile, a power of attorney is a legal document that grants someone the authority to act on your behalf in legal or financial matters. This becomes particularly important if you are incapacitated and unable to make decisions. Each of these terms plays a significant role in how an estate is managed and ultimately settled, so it's vital to grasp their meanings and implications.

To bring these terms to life, consider a family scenario where a sudden passing leaves the estate without a clear plan. If someone dies intestate, which means without a will, the distribution of their assets falls to the state's intestacy laws. Imagine a scenario where a parent passes away unexpectedly without a will, leaving behind a spouse and children from a previous marriage.

8

In such a case, the state will determine how assets are divided, which may not align with the deceased's wishes or family dynamics. This often leads to disputes and financial strain, underscoring the importance of having a clear estate plan and understanding the terminology that governs it.

Understanding legal jargon is not just about knowing definitions; it's about ensuring clarity in your estate planning process. Misunderstandings can lead to costly errors and family conflicts, which are often preventable with clear communication. When you understand the language of estate planning, you can articulate your wishes more precisely and engage more effectively with legal advisors. This knowledge empowers you to ask informed questions and make decisions that reflect your true intentions, reducing the risk of misinterpretation or oversight.

For those eager to deepen their understanding of estate planning terminology, numerous resources are available. Online legal dictionaries provide quick definitions and context for unfamiliar terms. Estate planning workshops offer interactive ways to learn, often featuring experts who can answer questions and provide practical advice. Books dedicated to estate planning can also serve as valuable references, offering detailed explanations and real-world examples. These resources can equip you with the knowledge you need to approach estate planning with confidence and clarity.

1.6 The Importance of Starting Early: Securing Your Legacy

The notion of planning for the future can often feel overwhelming, particularly when the future seems distant or uncertain. However, the advantages of starting your estate planning early are numerous and significant. By engaging in this process sooner rather than later, you gain more control over the outcomes that shape your legacy. Early planning allows you to articulate your wishes clearly, ensuring they are carried out as you want. It grants you the flexibility to adjust plans over time, accommodating changes in family dynamics, financial circumstances, or personal preferences. This adaptability is crucial because life is unpredictable and circumstances can shift rapidly.

Despite these benefits, many people hesitate to embark on estate planning at a young age or when they perceive their assets as modest. Common objections include feeling too young to need a plan or believing that estate planning is only relevant for those with substantial wealth. Yet, these assumptions miss the essence of estate planning, which is inherently dynamic. It's not a static, one-time event but a process that evolves with you, growing and adapting as your life unfolds. Early planning lays the groundwork for future wealth accumulation and ensures that even modest assets are protected and directed according to your wishes.

Certain life events serve as natural catalysts for estate planning, signaling the need to establish or update your plan. The birth of a child is one such moment when the responsibility of parenthood necessitates considerations for guardianship and financial provision. Similarly, purchasing a home represents a significant investment that should be protected within an estate plan. Even an overseas trip, with all its potential risks, can highlight the importance of having your affairs in order. Each of these milestones underscores the need for a comprehensive plan that accounts for your evolving life and priorities.

The long-term benefits of early estate planning are profound. It provides continued peace of mind, knowing that your loved ones are cared for and your wishes are documented. This foresight simplifies decision-making in times of emergency, reducing stress and uncertainty for your family. With a clear plan in place, your loved ones can focus on healing and remembering, rather than navigating complex legal and financial challenges. Over time, a well-considered plan can also lead to significant financial benefits, such as reduced taxes and preserved wealth, further securing your family's future.

Starting early in the estate planning process is not merely prudent; it is empowering. It is a proactive step that reflects a commitment to your legacy and the well-being of your loved ones. By taking control of this aspect of your life, you create a foundation that supports your goals and values, both now and in the years to come. As you continue to explore the intricacies of estate planning, remember that the decisions you make today will echo through the lives of those you care about, offering them stability and reassurance.

Don't move on to the next chapter without doing the following;

1. Do you have a will or trust?

- If not, you don't need to create it right now but have a think about what you want to leave and to whom. Start creating a list of your assets and who you want to pass them to. I'll cover how to get this done in upcoming chapters but it's worth getting started now
- If you do, is it up to date? Does your executor have a copy and do your family know where it is situated?

Chapter 2

Tailoring Your Estate Plan to Fit Your Needs

When you think about your family, what comes to mind? For many, it's a vibrant tapestry woven from diverse threads, each representing a unique relationship and history. This tapestry is especially intricate in blended and non-traditional families, where love and commitment often stretch beyond traditional boundaries. As you navigate estate planning, these rich family dynamics introduce complexities that require careful consideration and thoughtful solutions. Estate planning for such families isn't just about dividing assets; it involves honoring connections and ensuring everyone feels valued and respected.

2.1 Estate Planning for Blended and Non-Traditional Families

In blended families, where multiple marriages and stepchildren are part of the picture, the path to equitable estate planning can be fraught with challenges. Consider the scenario where you have children from previous marriages, each with varying needs and expectations. Without a well-structured plan, you might inadvertently leave some family members feeling overlooked or resentful. Similarly, cohabitating partners without legal marriage may face difficulties if one partner passes without clear instructions in place. These situations highlight the unique dynamics at play, underscoring the need for a tailored approach that reflects the intricacies of your family structure.

To ensure fair distribution among family members, several strategies can be employed. One effective method is creating specific trusts for each branch of your family. This allows you to allocate assets in a way that acknowledges the distinct roles and relationships within your family. For instance, separate trusts can be established for children from a first marriage and those from a second, ensuring that each group receives what you intend. Additionally, life insurance can serve as a valuable tool to equalize inheritances, providing a financial cushion that can be directed to specific beneficiaries. This ensures that each member of your family is treated fairly, minimizing potential disputes and fostering harmony.

Legal tools are invaluable in addressing the complex dynamics of blended and non-traditional families. Family settlement agreements, for example, can be drafted to outline specific arrangements and intentions, providing clarity and reducing the risk of misunderstandings. Customized will clauses allow you to specify unique conditions or distributions that reflect your family's particular needs. These instruments are designed to respect the individuality of your family while ensuring that your wishes are legally binding and clear to all involved.

Real-world examples illuminate the power of thoughtful estate planning in diverse families. Consider a blended family where the parents, each with children from previous marriages, faced potential conflicts over inheritance. By establishing tailored trusts and involving all family members in the planning process, they successfully resolved potential disputes before they could arise. In another case, a non-traditional family, where partners lived together without formal marriage, used a trust to ensure equitable distribution of assets, safeguarding the surviving partner's financial security. These scenarios underscore the importance of proactive planning and the peace it can bring to complex family situations.

Reflection Section

Take a moment to reflect on your own family dynamics. Consider the relationships that are most important to you and how they might influence your estate planning decisions. Jot down any specific concerns or goals you have regarding the distribution of your assets. This exercise can serve as a foundation for more in-depth discussions with your loved ones and advisors, helping to ensure that your estate plan truly reflects the unique tapestry of your family.

2.2 Guardianship for Minor Children: Ensuring Their Future

Choosing the right guardian for your minor children is one of the most profound decisions you will make in your estate planning journey. It involves considering who will best uphold your family values, provide a nurturing environment, and ensure your children's well-being. When selecting a guardian, you must assess their lifestyle and how it aligns with your own. Consider their parenting style, moral values, and the kind of life they lead. Financial stability is equally crucial. The ideal guardian should have the resources or capability to manage their own finances responsibly, as well as any potential inheritance your children may receive. It's a delicate balance, finding someone who can offer love, guidance, and financial security, ensuring your children grow up in a stable and supportive environment.

The legal process of appointing a guardian involves more than just a conversation with a trusted friend or family member. It requires a formal declaration within your estate documents. This typically begins with drafting a guardianship clause in your will, clearly stating who you wish to assume this vital role. It's essential to include detailed provisions that outline your expectations and any specific instructions regarding your children's upbringing. Once your will is drafted, you must ensure that it meets the legal requirements of your jurisdiction, which often involves court approval.

This step is crucial to validate your choice and prevent legal challenges. By formalizing your selection, you eliminate ambiguity and provide a clear path forward should the unthinkable occur.

Contingency planning is an important aspect of guardianship arrangements. Life is unpredictable, and it's wise to prepare for various scenarios. Designating alternate guardians provides a backup plan if your primary choice cannot fulfill their duties due to unforeseen circumstances. Regularly reviewing your guardianship decisions ensures they remain relevant and reflective of your current wishes. Circumstances change, and your appointed guardian's situation might evolve, making it necessary to revisit your selection periodically. This proactive approach ensures that your children will always have a designated caretaker who is willing and able to step in when needed, providing continuity and stability in their lives.

To illustrate the impact of thoughtful guardianship planning, consider the story of a family who faced the sudden loss of both parents due to an accident. Because they had meticulously planned for such an eventuality, their chosen guardians were able to step in immediately, providing the children with a seamless transition during an incredibly challenging time. The guardianship clause in the will left no room for doubt, and the court swiftly approved their appointment, minimizing disruption in the children's lives. Additionally, the parents had set aside education funds, ensuring that their children's academic futures were secure, regardless of the family's financial situation. This foresight not only alleviated financial concerns but also allowed the guardians to focus on emotional support and stability for the children.

In another instance, a couple named their close friend as the guardian for their daughter. When an unexpected illness rendered the original guardian unable to fulfill the role, the couple's alternate choice was ready to step in, thanks to the foresight of including a backup plan in their estate documents. This decision proved invaluable, as the alternate guardian was already familiar with the family's values and expectations, providing continuity and reassurance during a difficult transition. These examples underscore the importance of comprehensive guardianship planning, highlighting how proactive measures can safeguard your children's futures and bring peace of mind to everyone involved.

2.3 High-Net-Worth Estate Strategies: Protecting Large Estates

When you're managing substantial wealth, the stakes in estate planning are significantly heightened. One of the cornerstones of protecting a large estate is the strategic use of irrevocable trusts. These are powerful tools designed to shield assets from creditors and legal claims, ensuring that your wealth is preserved for future generations. By transferring assets into an irrevocable trust, you effectively remove them from your taxable estate, which can result in considerable tax savings. This move requires relinquishing control over the assets, but the trade-off is a robust layer of protection that can safeguard your estate from unforeseen liabilities. These trusts generally come into existence after you pass away and all your assets moved to be owned by this trust and won't be subject to estate taxes. If you have a large asset portfolio the tax savings are huge. It is more expensive than a will to set up but has significant tax savings at the back end.

Family limited partnerships (FLPs) offer another sophisticated method for asset protection. They allow you to maintain control over your assets while transferring ownership interest to family members. This strategy not only aids in minimizing estate taxes but also facilitates the gradual transfer of wealth to the next generation, thereby ensuring that your financial legacy is preserved. By creating an FLP, you consolidate family assets under a single legal entity, providing a structured way to manage and protect them. This approach also offers a degree of privacy, as FLPs are not required to disclose their holdings publicly, unlike individual estates. Upon your passing, it is exempt from estate taxes but during it's existence may be subject to income taxes.

Minimizing estate taxes is a critical concern for high-net-worth individuals, and there are effective strategies to address this. Charitable remainder trusts (CRTs) are one such tactic. By placing assets into a CRT, you can reduce taxable income through charitable deductions while simultaneously providing a steady income stream. Upon termination of the trust, the remaining assets are donated to a charity of your choice, aligning your philanthropic goals with tax efficiency. Additionally, gifting strategies can significantly lower your taxable estate. By making annual gifts to family members up to the IRS exclusion limit, you can gradually reduce the size of your estate, thus minimizing potential estate taxes. This approach not only benefits your heirs sooner but also allows you to witness the impact of your generosity during your lifetime.

For business owners, succession planning is a vital component of estate strategy. Buy-sell agreements are essential in ensuring a smooth transition of business ownership. These agreements stipulate the terms under which ownership interests can be transferred, often funded by life insurance policies. This arrangement protects the business from potential disruptions caused by the untimely passing of an owner, ensuring continuity and stability. Key person insurance is another vital tool, providing financial compensation to the business in the event of the loss of a critical team member. This insurance helps maintain operations and provides a buffer during the transition period, safeguarding the business's future.

Consider the story of a family business that has thrived across generations, thanks to strategic estate planning. This family utilized a combination of irrevocable trusts and FLPs to protect their wealth and ensure seamless succession. By implementing buy-sell agreements and key person insurance, they maintained business stability, allowing the company to flourish despite unforeseen challenges. In another instance, a high-net-worth individual successfully minimized estate taxes through strategic gifting and the establishment of charitable remainder trusts. This approach not only preserved the family's wealth but also supported charitable causes close to their hearts, creating a legacy of generosity and impact. These examples highlight the importance of thoughtful planning and the transformative potential of effective estate strategies for high-net-worth individuals.

2.4 Business Succession Planning: Ensuring Smooth Transitions

Imagine the business you've built over the years, the one you've poured your heart and soul into, continuing to thrive even when you're no longer at the helm. For business owners, succession planning is not just about passing the baton; it's about securing the legacy of hard work and dedication. The future transition of your enterprise is crucial for maintaining stability and protecting the livelihoods of your employees, who have become like family. Without a well-thought-out plan, the business could face uncertainty, putting both its operations and the jobs it supports at risk. This is why succession planning is indispensable. It ensures a seamless handover, preserving the business's core values and operational continuity while safeguarding the welfare of those who depend on it.

A comprehensive succession plan involves several key components. First, identifying potential successors is critical. This task requires evaluating the skills, experience, and leadership qualities of those who might take over. Whether it's a family member who understands the business' ethos or a trusted employee who has demonstrated capability, choosing the right successor is paramount. Next, the valuation of the business is essential. A clear understanding of the business' worth not only aids in determining fair compensation for ownership transfer but also helps in planning for future growth and investment. Regular valuation updates ensure that the business remains aligned with market conditions, providing a realistic picture of its financial health.

Transition strategies offer various paths for transferring business ownership. One approach is the gradual transfer of control, which allows the successor to learn the ropes over time. This phased transition can ease the shift for both the new leader and the staff, minimizing disruptions. Alternatively, the sale to third parties is an option when internal succession isn't feasible. This path might attract outside investors who bring fresh perspectives and resources. Family succession, on the other hand, keeps the business within the family, preserving its legacy across generations. Each strategy has its merits, and the choice depends on the unique circumstances and goals of the business owner.

Consider the story of a family-owned restaurant that successfully passed down through generations. The owners had a clear plan in place, selecting a successor years before retirement. This allowed for mentorship and gradual transfer of responsibilities, ensuring that the business continued to flourish with a fresh yet familiar leadership style. In another case, an employee buyout preserved a company's culture when the owner decided to retire. By selling shares to loyal employees, the business maintained its core values and operational ethos, benefiting from the team's deep understanding and commitment. These narratives highlight the effectiveness of thoughtful succession planning, showcasing the diverse approaches available to business owners.

2.5 Equitable Asset Distribution: Balancing Family Dynamics

In the delicate dance of estate planning, ensuring equitable asset distribution often presents a significant challenge. Families, by their very nature, are diverse and dynamic, each member carrying unique expectations and needs that can complicate the process. Imagine the emotional complexity when dividing a lifetime of memories and possessions. Heirs may have differing financial situations or personal aspirations, leading to varied perceptions of what is fair. These differences can create tension, especially when sentimental items like family heirlooms come into play. Such items often carry more emotional weight than monetary value, yet they can become the focal point of disputes if not addressed thoughtfully. It's not uncommon for one heir to cherish a piece of jewelry simply for its connection to a beloved relative, while another sees it as an asset to be liquidated for financial gain.

To navigate these complexities, several tools can facilitate balanced asset division. Equalization payments are one such instrument. They allow you to compensate heirs who receive less tangible assets by providing them with a monetary gift, thus maintaining equilibrium in the overall inheritance. This strategy is particularly useful when one heir receives a significant asset, such as a family home, which cannot be easily divided. Joint ownership agreements can also offer a solution, especially for assets like vacation properties or businesses. By granting multiple heirs shared ownership, you can ensure that each has a stake in preserving and enjoying the asset. These agreements require clear terms and conditions to prevent future conflicts, but they provide a framework for cooperative management.

Open communication is crucial in managing expectations and preventing misunderstandings during the distribution process. Family meetings, although sometimes challenging, provide a platform for discussing inheritance plans openly. By explaining your intentions and listening to concerns, you cultivate an environment of transparency and mutual respect. These discussions can be difficult, particularly if there are unresolved family dynamics or if the topic of estate planning has previously been taboo. In such cases, mediators can play a pivotal role. These neutral parties facilitate dialogue, helping families navigate emotionally charged conversations and reach amicable solutions. It's vital to reiterate that these are your wishes, ensuring that your voice guides the process even in your absence.

Consider a family grappling with the decision of what to do with the family home. The property, rich with memories, is desired by multiple heirs for different reasons. Through a series of family meetings, facilitated by a mediator, they agree to a joint ownership arrangement. This decision allows them to preserve the home as a shared retreat, maintaining its presence in the family for future generations. In another scenario, a trust is established to balance inheritance among siblings with disparate financial needs. By placing assets into a trust, the family ensures that each sibling receives fair support, tailored to their circumstances. These examples highlight how thoughtful planning and open dialogue can resolve potential conflicts and honor the diverse needs within a family.

2.6 Navigating Unique Cultural and Regional Considerations

Estate planning is deeply personal, and cultural backgrounds can profoundly influence the choices you make. In many cultures, family hierarchy and the respect for elders play a significant role in how assets are divided. For example, in some Asian families, the eldest son might traditionally inherit the family business or home, reflecting a longstanding cultural norm of passing leadership and responsibility to the next generation. This respect for hierarchy can influence not only the way assets are divided but also how decisions are made, with elders often consulted and given the final say. Similarly, cultural traditions can dictate specific bequests, such as leaving certain heirlooms to particular family members or making donations to community organizations that align with family values.

Regional legal variations further complicate estate planning. The differences between community property states and common law states, for instance, can significantly affect how your property is divided upon death. In community property states, assets acquired during marriage are generally considered jointly owned and are divided equally, regardless of whose name is on the title. This can impact your estate plan, especially if you have children from a previous marriage or personal assets you wish to keep separate. In contrast, common law states allow for more flexibility, where assets are owned by the individual whose name is on the title, giving you more control over how they are distributed. Similarly, inheritance laws can vary widely, with some regions imposing strict rules about who can inherit and in what proportions, which might not align with your personal wishes.

Tailoring your estate plan to fit these cultural and regional contexts requires sensitivity and foresight. Incorporating cultural values into your will can ensure that your estate plan reflects the traditions and priorities that are important to you and your family. This might involve specifying certain cultural practices to be observed after your passing or allocating funds to support cultural or religious events. Additionally, adjusting your plan to account for regional tax differences can help maximize the value of your estate.

Some states have their own estate or inheritance taxes, which can be mitigated through careful planning and strategic asset allocation.

Consider the case of a family with deep religious roots, where inheritance laws dictate specific distributions. By incorporating these religious principles into their estate plan, they ensure compliance with their beliefs while minimizing potential conflicts. Another example might involve a family from a region with significant estate taxes, who strategically gifts assets during their lifetime to reduce the taxable portion of their estate. These examples highlight the importance of culturally sensitive planning, demonstrating how a well-considered approach can honor traditions and optimize financial outcomes.

In conclusion, estate planning is not a one-size-fits-all process. It requires an understanding of the unique cultural and regional factors that influence your choices. By acknowledging these influences and tailoring your plan accordingly, you can create an estate strategy that respects your heritage, aligns with local laws, and meets your family's needs. Getting advice from an estate planning lawyer and financial advisor is important as a lot of these tax laws and trusts are complex and differ for each state. They know all of this information and work with it every day. In a later chapter, we'll talk about how to find a good estate planning lawyer. As we move forward, we'll explore how to maintain and update these plans to ensure they remain relevant and effective.

Don't move on to the next chapter without doing the following;

1. Do you have guardianship covered in your will/trust? If not consider who you would want to parent your children in your absence. Do they have the same or similar values to you? Will your child be happy to live with them? Will you leave enough money for your child to be financially secure? Have you communicated this to your guardians?

2. Do you have a backup guardian? Is it worth having a backup noted in your will/trust?

3. Could an irrevocable trust be appropriate for you? Contact an estate planning lawyer to discuss this

4. Have you considered all of the cultural, religious, and blended family dynamics in your will/trust? Write what you want down and an estate lawyer can tell you the best legal vehicle to make it happen and the tax impact of it

5. Have you considered how you want your business to be run when you pass? Will a family member buy it from you or will you gift it to them? If no family member is interested, how will you value the business to sell before you pass or in the event of your passing?

Chapter 3

Avoiding Common Pitfalls and Mistakes

Imagine building a house. You wouldn't want to start construction without a blueprint or a solid foundation, right? Estate planning works much the same way. A clear plan is crucial to ensure that your wishes are honored and your loved ones are cared for. Yet, many misconceptions can lead us astray, leaving our financial and familial foundations shaky. Let's explore some of these myths and understand how they can hinder effective planning.

One of the most pervasive myths is that estate planning is only for the wealthy. This misconception can lead many to dismiss the importance of having a plan in place. In reality, estate planning is essential for everyone, regardless of wealth or age. It's not just about distributing wealth; it's about making critical decisions regarding healthcare, guardianship, and end-of-life wishes. Without a plan, even modest estates can face legal challenges, causing unnecessary stress for those left behind. Consider the scenario where a single parent, without vast assets, unexpectedly passes away without a will. The lack of a clear directive can lead to lengthy legal battles over guardianship, leaving children in limbo during an already traumatic time.

Another common misconception is the belief that a will is all you need. While a will is a fundamental component of any estate plan, it doesn't cover everything. A comprehensive estate plan includes a variety of documents, such as trusts, healthcare directives, and powers of attorney. These elements work together to ensure that all aspects of your life and wishes are addressed. Relying solely on a will can leave significant gaps, especially if you have specific healthcare preferences or wish to avoid probate. Probate, often a lengthy and public process, can delay the distribution of assets and increase costs. Without additional planning, even with a will in place, families can find themselves embroiled in disputes or facing unexpected tax burdens.

Believing these myths can have tangible, negative consequences. Inadequate planning often leads to family disputes, as relatives may have differing interpretations of your wishes or expectations of their inheritances. These conflicts can fracture family relationships, sometimes irreparably. Additionally, without strategic planning, your estate may incur higher taxes, reducing the amount left for your heirs. Many are surprised to learn that estate taxes can apply even to estates they considered modest, especially in states with lower tax thresholds. This oversight can lead to heirs receiving far less than anticipated, causing financial strain.

Understanding the truth about estate planning can help dispel these myths. Planning is crucial for everyone, not just those with substantial wealth. It's about ensuring that your wishes are documented and honored, providing peace of mind for you and your loved ones. The role of comprehensive estate planning extends beyond a simple will. It encompasses a holistic approach to managing your affairs and protecting your family's future.

Real-life examples underscore the importance of dispelling these myths. Take, for instance, a family who assumed their modest estate didn't require detailed planning. When the parents passed unexpectedly, their children faced a protracted legal process to settle the estate, resulting in significant legal fees and strained relationships. In another example, an individual with a simple will left their heirs with unexpected tax obligations, as the will didn't address state-specific tax laws. Moreover, consider the case of children left without a known guardian because their parents believed estate planning was unnecessary until later in life. These scenarios highlight the risks of relying on misconceptions and the value of proactive, informed planning.

Reflection Section

Think about your own understanding of estate planning. Have any of these myths influenced your perceptions or decisions? Take a moment to consider the implications of these misconceptions on your plans. Reflect on any areas where you might need to seek additional information or make adjustments to ensure your estate plan is comprehensive and reflective of your true wishes.

3.1 Avoiding Probate: Strategies and Benefits

Probate often conjures images of endless legal proceedings and unnecessary stress. This process, while intended to ensure a fair distribution of assets, can become a cumbersome ordeal. One of its primary drawbacks is the time it consumes, which can delay the distribution of assets to your heirs. Families may find themselves waiting months, or even years, for the court to settle the estate. During this time, the estate remains in limbo, unable to be used to support the family or settle debts. Another significant downside is the public exposure that comes with probate. The process involves public records, meaning anyone can access sensitive details about your estate, which many would prefer to keep private. For those who value discretion, this level of transparency can be unsettling, as it exposes financial matters, potentially leading to unwanted scrutiny or disputes within the family.

Given these challenges, many seek to bypass probate altogether, and fortunately, there are effective strategies to do so. Establishing a revocable living trust is one popular method. When you transfer your assets into a trust, you essentially own them through the trust, allowing for seamless management and distribution upon your death without the need for probate. This strategy not only saves time but also keeps your financial dealings private. Another practical option is joint ownership of assets. By jointly titling property or accounts with rights of survivorship, these assets automatically pass to the surviving co-owner, sidestepping the probate process entirely. This approach is straightforward and ensures that your assets are quickly accessible to your loved ones when they need them most. Additionally, naming beneficiaries directly on accounts such as retirement funds or life insurance policies can also help avoid probate. When beneficiaries are clearly designated, these assets transfer directly to them, cutting through the red tape and providing immediate access.

The benefits of avoiding probate are substantial. With faster settlements, your family can access the resources they need without unnecessary delay. This can be crucial in maintaining their standard of living or covering urgent expenses, such as mortgage payments or education costs. Avoiding probate also preserves family privacy, allowing the details of your estate to remain confidential. Without the public record aspect of probate, your financial affairs stay within the family, reducing the risk of disputes over who inherits what. This privacy can be invaluable in maintaining harmony and preventing conflicts that often arise from misunderstandings or perceived unfairness.

Consider the story of a family that wisely chose to set up a living trust. When the family patriarch passed, the transition of assets was seamless, and the family avoided the drawn-out probate process altogether. The trust ensured that specific assets were distributed according to his wishes, with no room for ambiguity or contestation. This foresight allowed the family to focus on healing and supporting each other, rather than getting entangled in legal proceedings. In another scenario, a couple had the foresight to list each other as joint owners of their primary assets. When one partner passed away, the surviving spouse had immediate access to all shared assets, enabling them to manage day-to-day expenses without delay. This swift transition was a relief during an emotionally challenging time, illustrating the peace of mind that strategic planning can provide.

These examples highlight the advantages of avoiding probate through proactive planning. By taking steps to bypass this process, you can ensure a smoother, more private transition of your estate, sparing your loved ones from additional stress and uncertainty during a difficult time.

3.2 Common Mistakes in Will Creation and How to Avoid Them

Creating a will is a significant step in securing your family's future, yet it's easy to overlook some common pitfalls that can undermine your intentions. One frequent mistake is failing to update your will regularly. Life is ever-changing, and your will should reflect those changes. Whether it's the birth of a child, a marriage, or a shift in financial circumstances, your will needs to evolve with your life. Neglecting these updates can lead to outdated directives, inadvertently benefiting individuals you no longer wish to include or omitting new loved ones entirely. Imagine the turmoil of a will that still names a former spouse as the primary beneficiary while excluding a new partner or child. Such oversights can cause distress and conflict among those you care about most.

Another critical oversight is neglecting digital assets. As our lives become more intertwined with technology, digital assets—from online banking accounts to social media profiles—can hold significant value. Despite this, many wills fail to include provisions for these assets, leaving them inaccessible or lost. In a world where digital presence is part of our every day, forgetting to document login details, passwords, and specific wishes for these assets can result in them being overlooked entirely. This not only denies access to potentially valuable resources but also leaves a gap in your legacy, with digital memories and materials potentially lost forever.

The importance of proper witnessing cannot be overstated. A will that isn't witnessed correctly may be deemed invalid, regardless of its content. This procedural mistake can nullify your intentions, placing your estate into intestacy, where state laws dictate distribution rather than your wishes. The consequences can be dire, with heirs facing lengthy legal battles to assert their claims, often leading to family disputes and strained relationships. Without the safeguard of a valid will, your assets may end up in the hands of unintended beneficiaries, contrary to your plans.

To avoid these pitfalls, it's crucial to schedule regular reviews of your will. Setting a routine, such as reviewing your will annually or following major life events, ensures that it remains current and reflective of your wishes.

Including detailed instructions for digital assets within your will is also vital. Clearly specify how these should be managed or transferred upon your passing, providing necessary access details to a trusted individual. This foresight ensures that your digital legacy is preserved and managed according to your desires. Additionally, ensure that your will is witnessed according to legal standards, typically requiring the presence of two impartial witnesses. This simple yet vital step solidifies the validity of your will, safeguarding your intentions against legal challenges.

Consider the cautionary tale of a family whose patriarch failed to update his will after several significant life changes. His original will, drafted decades ago, named his siblings as beneficiaries, despite having a new family of his own. Upon his passing, the outdated will led to a protracted legal dispute between his wife and siblings, fracturing family bonds and consuming resources that could have been more constructively utilized. In another instance, a tech-savvy individual's failure to document digital assets resulted in the loss of valuable cryptocurrency holdings and cherished digital memories, leaving heirs unable to recover these intangible treasures. These stories serve as poignant reminders of the importance of vigilance and foresight in will creation.

3.3 Understanding Tax Implications and Strategies

Navigating the labyrinth of estate taxes can seem daunting, yet understanding their implications is crucial for a robust estate plan. At the federal level, estate taxes apply to the transfer of property at death, with a current threshold allowing individuals to pass up to $13.99 million tax-free. This exemption is scheduled to drop significantly after 2025, which could broaden the tax's impact. However, state-specific estate taxes can further complicate matters. Some states impose their own taxes, often with lower thresholds than the federal level. This means that even if your estate falls below the federal exemption, you could still face state estate taxes. Ignoring these variations can lead to costly surprises for your heirs, diminishing their inheritance and potentially causing financial strain during an already difficult time.

To mitigate these tax burdens, several strategies can be employed. One effective method is gifting during your lifetime. By transferring assets to your heirs while you're still alive, you can reduce the size of your taxable estate. The annual exclusion limit for gifts is currently $17,000 per recipient, allowing you to give substantial sums over time without incurring gift taxes. This approach not only lowers your estate's value but also allows you to witness the benefits of your generosity firsthand. Another powerful tool is setting up charitable trusts. These trusts can provide income to heirs while eventually transferring the remaining assets to a charity. This not only fulfills philanthropic goals but also offers significant tax deductions, reducing the taxable estate further. Structuring these arrangements requires careful planning, as they must align with both your financial goals and charitable intentions.

Even with these strategies, pitfalls abound, and missteps can be costly. A common error is misinterpreting tax laws, which can lead to unforeseen liabilities. Tax regulations are complex and frequently change, making it vital to stay informed and consult with knowledgeable advisors. Overlooking state estate taxes is another risk, as many assume that meeting federal requirements suffices. Each state has its own set of rules, and failure to account for them can result in substantial penalties. Avoiding these pitfalls requires diligence and a proactive approach, ensuring that your plan remains compliant and optimized for current tax laws.

Consider the example of a family who successfully reduced their tax liabilities through strategic gifting. Over several years, they transferred a portion of their wealth to their children, significantly lowering the estate's taxable value. This foresight not only preserved more of their legacy for future generations but also strengthened family bonds through shared experiences and support. In contrast, another family effectively utilized trusts to manage tax exposure. By setting up a charitable remainder trust, they minimized their estate tax while supporting causes they cared about deeply. This dual benefit underscored the power of thoughtful planning, demonstrating how strategic use of trusts can align financial and philanthropic goals seamlessly. These examples highlight the importance of understanding and actively managing the tax implications of your estate plan.

3.4 Choosing the Right Legal and Financial Advisors

Navigating the complexities of estate planning can feel overwhelming, but you're not alone in this endeavor. Professional advice is invaluable, ensuring that every legal and financial aspect of your estate plan is handled with precision. Expert guidance is crucial for maintaining legal compliance and navigating the intricate financial landscapes involved. Legal advisors are adept at drafting documents that comply with ever-changing laws, ensuring your intentions are clearly articulated and enforceable. Moreover, skilled financial advisors can help manage your assets, crafting strategies that align with your goals and mitigate potential tax liabilities. Their expertise can transform a daunting process into a manageable one, providing you with peace of mind.

Selecting the right professionals requires careful consideration. Start by checking credentials and experience. Look for advisors who specialize in estate planning, boasting certifications and years of practice in the field. This specialization ensures they have a deep understanding of the nuances involved. Referrals and testimonials are also valuable resources. Seek recommendations from trusted friends or family who have successfully navigated estate planning. Their firsthand experiences can guide you toward reputable advisors. Additionally, reading reviews or client testimonials can offer insights into an advisor's effectiveness and client satisfaction. These steps help you build a team of professionals who are not only qualified but also well-suited to your personal needs.

Each advisor plays a distinct role in the estate planning process. Lawyers are essential for drafting legal documents, such as wills, trusts, and powers of attorney. They ensure these documents are legally sound and reflect your wishes accurately. Their role is to provide clarity and prevent future disputes by addressing potential legal challenges proactively. On the other hand, financial advisors focus on managing your assets. They provide guidance on investment strategies, tax planning, and wealth preservation. Their goal is to maximize your estate's value while minimizing liabilities. By working together, these advisors create a comprehensive strategy that covers all bases, from legal compliance to financial optimization. If you find a good lawyer they may have a recommendation to a financial advisor who they work closely with and vice versa. Making sure they work as a team towards your goals is important.

Consider the story of a couple who successfully navigated their estate planning with the help of a skilled team. They began by seeking referrals from friends, which led them to an experienced lawyer and a savvy financial advisor. The lawyer meticulously drafted their documents, ensuring every detail aligned with their wishes. Meanwhile, the financial advisor developed a robust investment strategy that optimized their wealth while considering future tax implications. Together, this team crafted a seamless estate plan that reflected the couple's values and objectives. The complex nature of their estate was handled smoothly, with every potential issue addressed proactively. This collaboration not only protected their assets but also provided them with confidence, knowing their legacy was in good hands.

Another example involves a high-net-worth individual who faced the challenge of managing a multifaceted estate. With properties in multiple states and diverse investments, the complexity required a coordinated approach. By choosing advisors with specific expertise—in real estate, tax law, and investment management—the individual was able to streamline the process. Each advisor contributed their knowledge, from ensuring compliance with varied state laws to optimizing the tax strategy. The result was a cohesive estate plan that minimized liabilities and maximized the estate's potential. This tale underscores the importance of selecting professionals who can address the unique aspects of your estate, providing a tailored approach that meets your specific needs.

3.5 The Perils of Procrastination: Why Estate Planning Can't Wait

Life has a way of throwing curve balls when we least expect them. It's easy to push estate planning to the back burner, thinking there's always tomorrow. Yet, delaying these crucial decisions can leave you unprepared for unexpected events, turning life's unpredictability into a crisis. Imagine dealing with a sudden illness or an unforeseen accident without a plan in place. This unpreparedness can magnify stress, leaving your family to navigate a maze of legal and financial decisions in the midst of emotional turmoil. The absence of a plan can compound grief with confusion, complicating an already challenging time.

Life events often necessitate a fresh look at estate planning. Marriage or divorce, for instance, can dramatically alter your financial landscape and beneficiary designations. Failing to update your plan in these instances can lead to unintended parties receiving assets or loved ones being overlooked. The birth of children represents another pivotal moment. As parents, the instinct to protect and provide for your new child is strong, making it crucial to ensure your estate plan reflects this new responsibility. Overseas travel is another trigger for revisiting your plans. While travel is an exciting venture, it also carries inherent risks that make having your affairs in order a wise decision. Each of these life changes serves as a reminder of the importance of regularly updating and reviewing your estate plan.

Taking action now on your estate planning can offer profound peace of mind. Knowing your loved ones are protected and your wishes are clear can relieve anxiety and provide a sense of control over the future. A well-crafted plan offers flexibility, allowing you to adapt it as your life changes. This adaptability is crucial, given how quickly circumstances can evolve. By starting today, you give yourself the freedom to make informed decisions at your own pace, without the pressure of a looming deadline or an unexpected crisis forcing your hand.

Consider the story of a family blindsided by the sudden illness of their patriarch. Without an estate plan, chaos ensued as family members scrambled to manage his affairs, leading to costly mistakes and prolonged legal battles. The lack of foresight resulted in unnecessary stress and financial losses, which could have been avoided with proper planning. In another instance, a couple hastily assembled a plan when one partner fell ill. The rushed process led to overlooked details and legal challenges that could have been mitigated with earlier preparation. Similarly, a man who remarried later in life failed to update his will. Upon his death, his estate was distributed according to outdated wishes, leaving his new wife without support and igniting conflict among his children.

Procrastination in estate planning can have dire consequences. The absence of a plan can leave your family vulnerable, facing unnecessary hardships during times of distress. By acting now, you ensure that your legacy is one of security and provision, rather than disarray and uncertainty. As we conclude this chapter, remember that the steps you take today can protect your loved ones tomorrow. With these insights, you're better equipped to move forward confidently, knowing that your estate plan reflects your values and priorities.

Don't move on to the next chapter without doing the following;

1. When was the last time you updated your will/trust? Review it now and see if there's anything you need to update. Put in your diary a reminder in a year to review it again to keep your wishes current
2. If you haven't created a will/trust we'll cover how to find an estate lawyer in Chapter 5 but begin now by asking friends and family for recommendations for an estate lawyer and a good financial advisor

Chapter 4

Organizing and Documenting Your Assets

Imagine trying to solve a puzzle with pieces scattered all over the room. Without knowing what each piece represents and how they fit together, the task seems daunting. Similarly, estate planning involves organizing the pieces of your financial life into a coherent picture. This begins with creating a detailed inventory of your assets. Think of it as laying out the puzzle pieces so you can see what you have and where it fits in the larger scheme of your estate. A well-maintained inventory is crucial for effective estate planning, as it ensures that your assets are distributed according to your wishes and helps streamline the probate process, making it easier for your loved ones to manage your estate when the time comes.

The process of creating an inventory may seem overwhelming, but breaking it down into manageable steps can simplify it significantly. Start with your physical assets. List each item you own, from real estate properties to personal belongings like jewelry, art, and collectibles. These tangible assets often hold significant value and sentimental meaning, so it's important to document them thoroughly. Next, move on to financial assets, including stocks, bonds, savings accounts, and retirement funds. Be sure to include account numbers and contact information for financial institutions. This comprehensive list not only provides a clear picture of your wealth but also serves as a road map for your heirs, guiding them toward the assets they may inherit.

In today's digital age, numerous tools can aid in inventory management. Personal finance apps like Mint or YNAB offer platforms for tracking assets and expenses, providing an overview of your financial landscape at a glance. These tools can be particularly useful for organizing complex portfolios and ensuring that no asset is overlooked. Alternatively, spreadsheets such as those created in Microsoft Excel offer a customizable approach to inventory management, allowing you to tailor the format to your specific needs. For those who prefer a more hands-on approach, an estate planner workbook can serve as a tangible record of your assets, with sections dedicated to different asset types and personal notes. And if you want to store it online try Sortly which you would need to purchase, but keeps things like serial numbers and can be updated easily. These tools not only help in the initial creation of your inventory but also in maintaining it over time, ensuring it remains accurate and up-to-date.

Regularly updating your asset inventory is as important as creating it. As life evolves, so does your financial situation. Whether it's acquiring new assets, selling old ones, or experiencing changes in asset ownership, reflecting these updates in your inventory is crucial. Regular reviews ensure that your estate plan remains relevant and that your heirs have access to the most current information. This diligence can prevent confusion and disputes, providing peace of mind that your legacy is protected. Moreover, keeping your inventory current ensures that any changes in the value of your assets are accurately recorded, which can be vital for tax and probate purposes.

Reflection Section

Take a moment to consider the assets in your life. What items hold the most value to you, both financially and sentimentally? Begin an inventory by listing these assets, noting their significance and any specific instructions you might have for their distribution. Use this exercise as a starting point for deeper exploration, allowing you to build a comprehensive inventory that reflects your unique circumstances and priorities. This reflection can provide clarity and direction as you continue to develop your estate plan, ensuring that it aligns with your values and goals.

4.1 Essential Documents for Estate Planning

Navigating the intricacies of estate planning requires a firm grasp of several critical documents. At the heart of this process are wills and trusts, each serving a unique purpose in securing your legacy. A will is the cornerstone, outlining how your assets should be distributed after your passing and appointing guardians for any minor children. It provides a clear directive to ensure your wishes are honored, minimizing potential disputes among heirs. Meanwhile, trusts offer a way to manage your assets both during your life and after you're gone. They can help avoid probate, maintain privacy, and offer specific conditions under which your assets are distributed, which can be particularly useful in complex family situations or when maintaining control over the timing of distributions.

Powers of attorney are another vital component of your estate plan. This document grants a trusted individual the authority to make decisions on your behalf if you become incapacitated. There are generally two types: financial power of attorney and medical power of attorney. The former allows your agent to manage your financial affairs, ensuring bills are paid and investments are managed effectively. The latter enables your designated healthcare proxy to make medical decisions according to your preferences. These documents provide a safety net, ensuring that someone you trust will handle your affairs according to your wishes, even if you're unable to communicate them yourself.

Preparing these documents requires careful thought and precision. Consulting with legal professionals is highly recommended to ensure that your documents comply with state laws and accurately reflect your intentions. Different states have varying requirements for what makes a document legally valid, such as the number of witnesses needed or the necessity of notarization. A qualified lawyer can guide you through these requirements, helping to draft documents that stand up to legal scrutiny. It's also essential to review these documents periodically, particularly after significant life changes like marriage, divorce, or the birth of a child, to ensure they remain current and relevant.

To facilitate the assembly of these documents, a checklist can be invaluable. Start by verifying that all necessary signatures and notarizations are in place. This step is crucial for ensuring the legal validity of your documents. Next, consider where you'll store these documents. They should be kept in a secure yet accessible location, such as a fireproof safe or a safety deposit box or online in an encrypted digital vault. It's also wise to provide copies to your lawyer or a trusted family member, ensuring they can be accessed when needed. Keeping a record of where these documents are stored and who has access to them can prevent confusion and delays when they are required.

Checklist for Document Assembly

- Ensure all documents are signed and notarized as required by state law
- Store original documents in a secure, easily accessible location
- Provide copies to your lawyer or a trusted individual
- Keep a detailed record of document locations and access permissions

By taking these steps, you can ensure that your estate plan is both comprehensive and effective, providing peace of mind for you and your loved ones.

4.2 Using Technology to Manage and Protect Your Estate

In today's digital age, technology offers powerful tools to aid in managing and securing your estate plan. Imagine having all your essential documents organized and accessible with just a few clicks, all from the comfort of your home. Online platforms, like Google Drive, for document storage and sharing have revolutionized the way we handle estate planning, offering a centralized location where you can safely store wills, trusts, and other critical papers.

These platforms provide the convenience of accessing your documents from anywhere, ensuring you can update or reference them whenever needed. Digital vaults, another innovative solution, offer secure access to important information, allowing you to keep sensitive data such as account numbers and passwords protected yet readily available for those you trust.

Security is paramount when dealing with digital tools. Choosing reputable platforms with robust security features ensures your information remains private and protected. Two-factor authentication is a key feature offered by many services, adding an extra layer of security by requiring a second form of verification, such as a text message code or app notification. This means even if someone obtains your password, they cannot access your account without this additional verification step. Encrypted data storage, like Dropbox, further enhances security by converting your information into a code that is only accessible to those with the proper decryption key, safeguarding it from unauthorized access. These features are crucial in maintaining the integrity and confidentiality of your estate documents, giving you peace of mind that your sensitive information is secure.

The benefits of embracing digital estate management extend far beyond security. These tools enhance efficiency by allowing instant access to your documents from virtually any location, whether you're at home or traveling. This flexibility means you can make changes or share information with advisors quickly and easily, without the hassle of physical paperwork. Sharing access with your executor is another significant advantage. By granting them digital access, you ensure they have immediate access to the documents they need to fulfill their duties effectively, facilitating a smoother estate administration process. This ease of sharing reduces delays and streamlines communication, ensuring your estate plan is executed according to your wishes.

Consider the example of a family who utilized a digital vault to manage their estate documents. This family discovered the convenience and security of storing their wills, insurance policies, and financial records in a centralized, secure location. When the time came to execute the estate plan, the executor had immediate access to all necessary documents, allowing them to act swiftly and efficiently. This proactive approach prevented potential complications and ensured a seamless transition of assets. Another case involved an executor who benefited from shared online access to estate plans. By having digital access, they were able to collaborate with financial advisors and legal professionals in real time, making informed decisions that aligned with the deceased's wishes. Don't forget that even though the storage is digital the documents still need to be witnessed and properly executed. These examples illustrate the transformative impact of integrating technology into estate planning, demonstrating its potential to simplify and enhance the process for everyone involved.

4.3 Documenting Wishes: Healthcare Directives and More

Have you ever considered how you want to be cared for if you can't make decisions for yourself? Healthcare directives are a crucial part of estate planning, ensuring your medical wishes are honored when you can't speak for yourself. They offer peace of mind, knowing that your preferences will guide your care, whether you face a temporary setback or a long-term condition. Without these directives, your family might struggle with difficult decisions in emotionally charged situations. By having your wishes documented clearly, you relieve your loved ones of the burden of guessing or, worse, disagreeing over what you might have wanted.

Creating healthcare directives involves a few key steps. Begin by thinking about your treatment preferences in various scenarios. Do you want aggressive treatments, or do you prefer comfort-focused care? Once you have a clear sense of your wishes, appoint a healthcare proxy. This is someone you trust to make medical decisions on your behalf if you're unable to do so and this should be the person who is your medical power of attorney. It's wise to name a backup as well, in case your first choice is unavailable. Long-term healthcare preferences should also be considered, especially if you have strong feelings about your care in chronic or end-of-life situations. Write these preferences down in a way that's easy for your proxy to understand and implement. These documents must be properly executed to be valid so please consult your lawyer for the right advice.

Beyond healthcare proxies and treatment preferences, other directives are equally important. A living will or advanced healthcare directive, for example, outlines specific treatments you do or do not want. This might include decisions about life-sustaining measures, like ventilation or feeding tubes. A do-not-resuscitate (DNR) order is another directive you might consider, particularly if you wish to avoid CPR in the event of a cardiac arrest. These documents ensure that your healthcare providers and family members are on the same page, respecting your autonomy even when you're unable to communicate.

Consider the story of a patient who meticulously documented her healthcare wishes. When she faced a serious illness, her family knew exactly what steps to take because her directives were clear and well-communicated. This clarity allowed her family to focus on supporting her emotionally, rather than agonizing over medical decisions. In another scenario, a family avoided potential disputes because their loved one's healthcare power of attorney and DNR orders were well-established. The documents provided not only guidance but also comfort in knowing they were honoring their loved one's true wishes. These examples highlight the power of comprehensive healthcare planning, illustrating how it can prevent confusion and conflict during challenging times.

4.4 Digital Assets: Protecting Your Online Presence

In today's digital age, the landscape of personal assets has expanded beyond the tangible. We now possess digital assets, which have become an integral part of our lives. These include social media accounts, online banking profiles, investment accounts, and even digital currencies. It's crucial to include these in your estate plan because they hold both financial and sentimental value.

Consider your social media accounts—they are archives of memories and interactions with loved ones. Similarly, your online banking and investment accounts represent significant portions of your financial portfolio. Ignoring these assets in your estate planning can lead to lost opportunities and create challenges for your heirs.

Securing your digital assets begins with creating a comprehensive digital asset inventory. This inventory should list all your online accounts, including usernames, passwords, and the purpose of each account. It's essential to keep this inventory updated, reflecting any changes in account details or new accounts you may open. Using a password manager can greatly assist in this process. These tools not only help organize your passwords securely but also allow you to share access with trusted individuals without revealing sensitive information. This ensures that your digital assets are accessible to those you designate, protecting them from unauthorized access while maintaining your privacy.

When managing digital assets, it's important to understand the legal considerations that come into play. Different platforms have varying terms of service agreements, which can impact how your accounts are managed after your passing. Some services allow you to name a legacy contact who can manage your account, while others may automatically delete your profiles if left dormant for a specified period. Familiarizing yourself with these terms is crucial in ensuring your digital legacy is preserved according to your wishes. Digital estate planning services can also offer guidance and support, helping you navigate these complexities. These services provide expertise in managing digital assets, ensuring they are handled with care and legality in mind. Your lawyer should be able to recommend one for your state.

Success stories illustrate the effectiveness of proactive digital asset management. Take, for instance, a family who meticulously planned for the transfer of their online accounts. By maintaining a detailed digital asset inventory and using a password manager, they ensured seamless access to crucial financial accounts and cherished digital keepsakes. This foresight allowed them to navigate the complexities of digital asset management with ease, preserving the deceased's online presence and assets. In another example, a person's digital legacy was carefully curated through thoughtful planning. By understanding the terms of service agreements for each platform and leveraging digital estate planning services, they ensured their social media and online profiles continued to reflect their values and memories. These stories highlight the importance of including digital assets in your estate plan, illustrating how careful planning can protect and preserve your online presence for future generations.

4.5 Long-Term Storage Solutions: Keeping Your Documents Secure

Securing your estate planning documents is not merely a suggestion; it's a necessity. These papers hold the key to your legacy, detailing your wishes and ensuring your assets are managed and distributed as you intend. Without proper storage, these crucial documents are vulnerable to loss, damage, or unauthorized access. Imagine the turmoil if your will or trust documents were accidentally destroyed in a fire or misplaced during a move. This could lead to confusion, disputes, and even legal battles among your heirs. Securely storing these documents protects against such risks, providing peace of mind that your estate plan remains intact and accessible when needed.

There are several methods to store your documents securely, each with its own advantages. Safety deposit boxes at banks offer robust security against theft and environmental damage, providing a trustworthy option for those who prefer traditional storage methods. These boxes are ideal for storing original documents, as they are protected by the bank's security measures. However, access may be limited to bank hours, which could delay retrieval in emergencies. Fireproof home safes are another effective solution, offering immediate access while safeguarding documents from fire and water damage. They combine the convenience of home access with the security of protecting against physical threats. For those embracing digital transformation, cloud-based storage offers a modern alternative. This option allows you to store and access your documents from anywhere with an internet connection, ensuring they are safe from physical threats and can be shared easily with authorized individuals.

Choosing the right storage solution requires careful consideration of your personal needs and preferences. Weigh the pros and cons of physical versus digital storage. Physical storage, like safety deposit boxes and home safes, offers tangible security and protection against cyber threats but may limit access. Digital storage provides unparalleled convenience and ease of sharing but requires strong cybersecurity measures to protect against unauthorized access. Ensure that your executor and trusted family members have access to your stored documents. This is crucial in enabling them to execute your estate plan smoothly and without unnecessary delays. Consider providing them with instructions on how to access the documents, whether through a key, combination, or digital login credentials.

To illustrate the benefits of proper storage, consider a family who faced an unexpected emergency. Because they stored their estate documents in a fireproof home safe, they were able to retrieve them quickly, avoiding any delays in accessing critical information. This foresight allowed them to focus on their immediate needs without the added stress of searching for vital papers. In another instance, a family utilized cloud-based storage to keep their estate documents. When the time came to execute the estate plan, authorized family members accessed the documents seamlessly, ensuring a smooth transition and minimizing potential conflicts. These examples highlight how thoughtful storage decisions can prevent complications and provide assurance that your plans are both protected and accessible.

In securing your estate documents, you're not just guarding against loss or damage. You're ensuring that when the time comes, your wishes are honored efficiently and without unnecessary hurdles. Tailor your storage solutions to fit your lifestyle and the needs of your loved ones, creating a system that offers both security and accessibility. This proactive approach not only safeguards your legacy but also provides invaluable peace of mind for you and your family. As you continue to refine your estate plan, remember that a well-protected document is a vital part of a well-prepared plan.

Don't move on to the next chapter without doing the following;

1. Have you done a detailed asset listing? Also include a liability listing too
2. Did you list your digital assets in point 1? List out banking details, share account logins, social media logins and store in your secure digital vault
3. Have you considered who you will pass these assets and liabilities too? Start thinking about and allocating names
4. Do you have a healthcare directive in place? Consider creating one and communicating your wishes to your family. Ensure your healthcare proxy knows your wishes and has a copy of the directive and a medical power of attorney so they can show it when needed
5. Do you have a power of attorney in place? It is wise to do this as if you are ever incapacitated this document will enable your financial life will continue on while you are incapacitated

Chapter 5

Engaging Professional Help Wisely

Imagine finding yourself in a labyrinth, each turn more confusing than the last. You have a map, but it's written in a language that feels foreign. This is how many experience estate planning without professional guidance. The complexities of legal jargon and the nuances of law can leave even the most diligent planner feeling overwhelmed. Yet, this is a journey you don't have to undertake alone. Engaging the right professionals can transform this maze into a straightforward path, ensuring that your estate plan is not just a collection of documents but a solid foundation for your legacy.

5.1 When to Consult a Lawyer: Knowing Your Limits

There are key moments when seeking legal advice becomes essential to protect your interests and ensure your estate plan withstands scrutiny. Complex family dynamics, for instance, often require the clarity and precision that only a seasoned lawyer can provide. Consider a blended family where stepchildren and biological children have varied expectations and entitlements. Navigating such intricacies without expert guidance can lead to unintended exclusions or conflicts. A lawyer can help articulate your wishes clearly and legally, aligning them with your family's unique structure. Furthermore, significant changes in state or federal estate laws can alter the landscape of your planning. Laws evolve, often with little public fanfare, yet their impact can be profound. Legal professionals remain abreast of these changes, ensuring your estate plan remains compliant and effective.

While the allure of DIY estate planning, with its promise of saving time and money, might be tempting, the risks are substantial. Overlooking critical legal requirements is a common pitfall. A plan that seems thorough to the untrained eye might fail to meet essential legal standards, leaving your estate vulnerable to disputes or misinterpretation. Unintentionally creating legally invalid documents is a risk not worth taking. A will or trust that doesn't comply with state-specific legalities can be contested, or worse, declared void. This can result in your estate being distributed according to default laws, which might not reflect your wishes. The potential for error in DIY approaches is high, with consequences that could significantly impact your heirs.

The benefits of legal counsel extend beyond mere compliance. Lawyers tailor documents to fit specific legal contexts, ensuring that every detail aligns with your intentions and the law. This customization is invaluable, as it accounts for variables that generic templates cannot. Professional validation also provides peace of mind. Knowing that your estate plan has been meticulously reviewed by an expert offers reassurance that your legacy is secure. Legal professionals can simplify the process, demystifying complex legal terms and guide you through decisions with clarity and confidence.

Consider the story of a family facing a complex estate challenge. With multiple properties across state lines and a history of blended family dynamics, the potential for conflict was high. By engaging a skilled estate lawyer, they navigated these complexities seamlessly. The lawyer clarified inheritance rights and structured the estate plan to reflect the family's diverse needs, preventing disputes before they could arise. In another scenario, a couple sought legal advice to revise their estate plan following a significant law change. What seemed a minor adjustment to them had profound implications, and the lawyer's timely intervention prevented costly probate proceedings. These stories underscore the transformative role of legal professionals in crafting resilient estate plans.

Reflection Section

Reflect on your current estate plan, if you have one. Are there areas where you feel uncertain or overwhelmed? Consider if recent life changes or complex family dynamics might necessitate legal guidance. Use this section to note any questions or concerns you have about your estate plan's desired result. This reflection can serve as a starting point when consulting a legal professional to ensure your plan is robust and aligned with your intentions.

5.2 Interviewing Lawyers: Asking the Right Questions

Embarking on the process of estate planning is akin to crafting a masterpiece—each decision a deliberate brushstroke. Choosing the right lawyer to guide you is crucial, and preparing for your interview with potential lawyers can set the stage for a successful partnership. Begin by considering the specific nuances of your situation. Does the lawyer have experience with cases similar to yours? Whether you're navigating the complexities of a blended family or managing a business, their familiarity with such scenarios can be invaluable. Next, ensure they have a thorough understanding of state-specific estate laws. These laws can vary significantly, and a lawyer well-versed in your state's regulations can help avoid costly missteps.

Compatibility with your legal counsel is not just a bonus; it's a necessity. A comfortable, trusting relationship forms the backbone of effective collaboration. Pay attention to their communication style and responsiveness. Are they patient and clear in their explanations, or do you feel rushed and confused? Your lawyer should align with your personal values and goals, understanding not just your financial situation but also the principles that guide your decisions. This alignment fosters a productive relationship where you feel heard and respected, allowing you to navigate estate planning with confidence and clarity.

Red flags can indicate that a lawyer might not be the right fit for you, and recognizing these signs early can save time and resources. Be wary of those who are not transparent about fees. A good lawyer will offer clarity on their pricing structure, whether it involves hourly rates, flat fees, or retainer agreements. Ambiguity in this area can lead to unexpected costs. Also, assess their ability to provide clear explanations. If they struggle to explain complex legal terms in a way that makes sense to you, it may hinder your understanding and involvement in your own planning process. This lack of clarity can lead to miscommunication and dissatisfaction down the line.

One can find numerous stories highlighting the impact of asking the right questions during lawyer interviews. Consider a client who, during an initial consultation, discovered their lawyer's hidden expertise in estate tax law. This unexpected insight proved invaluable, as it allowed them to optimize their estate plan significantly, minimizing tax liabilities. This revelation only came about because the client took the time to delve into the lawyer's experience with specific tax issues. Another tale involves a client who built a strong foundation of trust through open and honest discussions with their lawyer. By addressing their concerns candidly and seeking a lawyer who was responsive and empathetic, they established a relationship that felt more like a partnership than a transaction. This rapport enabled them to navigate the estate planning process with ease and assurance, knowing they had an advocate who genuinely understood their needs.

These narratives underscore the importance of thorough preparation and open dialogue when interviewing potential lawyers. By approaching these conversations with a clear understanding of your needs and expectations, you can identify the professionals who are best suited to guide you through the estate planning process.

5.3 Understanding the Cost of Professional Services

Navigating the costs associated with estate planning can feel like walking through a financial labyrinth, especially when you're trying to make sense of the various fee structures. Typically, you'll encounter three primary billing methods: hourly rates, flat fees, and retainers. Hourly rates are straightforward, charging you for each hour a lawyer spends on your case. This can be unpredictable, as complex issues might require more time than anticipated. Be sure to ask for an estimate of how many hours they think they'll need so you have an idea of what the total cost may be. Flat fees, on the other hand, offer a set price for specific services, such as drafting a will or setting up a trust. This can provide peace of mind, knowing exactly what you'll pay upfront. Retainers work as advance payments, securing a lawyer's services by reserving a block of their time, while they deduct fees at their hourly rate from the retainer as work progresses. Understanding these structures helps you budget accordingly and choose a plan that aligns with your financial situation.

Keeping legal expenses in check doesn't mean sacrificing quality. Bundling services is one way to manage costs effectively. By grouping related services together, such as estate planning and tax advice, you might negotiate a discount, making complex planning more affordable. Also consider bundling power of attorney and healthcare directives/living sills too. Additionally, seeking quotes from multiple firms can help you compare rates and services. Don't hesitate to ask for detailed estimates and inquire about any additional costs that might arise. This transparency allows you to make informed decisions, ensuring you receive the best value for your investment. Remember, while saving money is important, it shouldn't come at the expense of quality or thoroughness in your estate planning. A well-executed plan can save significant amounts in the long run, avoiding costly legal disputes or errors.

When considering legal services, it's crucial to weigh the value of the service over mere cost. High-quality legal assistance ensures your estate plan is not only legally sound but also tailored to your specific needs. This bespoke approach can prevent future complications and provide long-term benefits. Comprehensive planning addresses both immediate needs and future contingencies, offering peace of mind that your affairs are in order. The value of these services becomes particularly apparent in complex estates, where the expertise and foresight of a skilled lawyer can safeguard your interests and enhance your legacy's longevity.

Every now and then, you hear about families who managed to secure affordable, yet effective, legal help. Take, for instance, a family that turned to a legal aid organization to craft their estate plan. Despite their modest means, they received expert guidance, ensuring their wishes were documented and legally binding. This proactive approach saved them from potential pitfalls and provided clarity to their heirs. In another case, a couple opted for early and proactive planning, which allowed them to spread out costs over time. By starting their planning early, they avoided a last-minute scramble, reducing the likelihood of errors and ensuring their plan was comprehensive and up-to-date. These stories underline that effective estate planning doesn't have to break the bank; with careful consideration and strategic choices, you can protect your legacy without overspending. I know some of these fees are a lot of money but it is a one-off exercise and it needs to be done and done well. Don't delay because of the cost, consider it a worthwhile investment to get your estate in order.

5.4 Collaborating with Financial Advisors for Estate Planning

Imagine trying to piece together a puzzle without knowing what the final picture looks like. Estate planning can feel like this, especially when it comes to understanding your financial landscape. This is where financial advisors come into play, offering invaluable guidance in managing and growing your assets while ensuring your estate plan is aligned with your financial goals. Their role goes beyond simple advice; they help craft a strategy that integrates asset management and investment strategies with tax planning and optimization. By carefully balancing these elements, they ensure that your estate plan not only reflects your wishes but also maximizes the financial health of your legacy.

The benefits of integrating financial advice into your estate planning process are manifold. A financial advisor provides a holistic view of your financial health, allowing you to see the bigger picture and how each piece fits together. This perspective is crucial when coordinating the legal and financial aspects of your estate plan. By working in tandem with your lawyer, a financial advisor ensures that your assets are structured in a way that supports your overall goals, whether it's minimizing tax liabilities or ensuring your heirs are provided for in a manner consistent with your values. This collaboration enhances the coherence and effectiveness of your estate plan, ensuring that nothing is left to chance.

Choosing the right financial advisor is a decision that requires careful consideration. Look for someone with the right credentials and certifications, such as a Certified Financial Planner (CFP) designation, which indicates a level of expertise and professionalism. Experience in estate and retirement planning is also crucial, as these advisors will have a deeper understanding of the unique challenges and opportunities that arise in these areas. It's important to find an advisor who not only has the technical skills but also the ability to communicate effectively and understand your personal goals. This alignment ensures that the advice they provide resonates with your vision and priorities.

Consider the stories of families who have successfully collaborated with financial advisors to enhance their estate plans. One family significantly increased their inheritance through smart investments guided by their advisor. By strategically reallocating assets and diversifying their portfolio, they were able to grow their wealth, ensuring a more substantial legacy for future generations. In another instance, a family faced daunting tax burdens due to the complexity of their estate. With the help of their financial advisor, they implemented strategic tax planning measures that reduced their liabilities, allowing them to preserve more of their wealth for their heirs. These examples underscore the transformative potential of thoughtful financial planning, illustrating how the right guidance can enhance and protect your estate.

5.5 The Role of Executors: Selecting and Guiding Them

When it comes to estate planning, choosing an executor is one of the most crucial decisions you will face. Executors are the linchpins in the estate administration process, tasked with a host of responsibilities that ensure your wishes are executed with precision. Their duties include managing the estate's administration, which involves inventorying assets, notifying creditors, and addressing any outstanding debts. Executors also oversee the complex task of asset distribution, ensuring that your beneficiaries receive their inheritances as specified in your will. This role requires a meticulous attention to detail and a steadfast commitment to honoring your intentions.

Selecting the right person for this pivotal role requires careful thought. Trustworthiness and integrity are paramount, as the executor will have access to sensitive financial information and must act in the best interests of the estate and its beneficiaries. The ability to handle pressure and conflict is equally important. Executors often face challenging situations, such as disputes among heirs or unexpected financial hurdles. Opt for someone who can remain calm and composed under stress, effectively mediating conflicts with diplomacy and fairness. Consider their organizational skills and financial acumen, as these attributes will aid them in navigating the often complex landscape of estate administration.

Once chosen, it is vital to prepare your executor for their role. Providing detailed instructions and access to necessary documents is a foundational step. This includes your will, any trusts, and pertinent financial records. Discussing expectations and potential challenges in advance can help your executor anticipate issues and devise strategies to address them. Open communication is key. Make sure your executor understands your values and goals, which will guide their decisions in ambiguous situations. This preparation not only equips them with the tools they need but also reassures them that they have your full confidence.

Consider the example of an executor who successfully managed an estate with multiple properties and varied investments. By maintaining clear communication with beneficiaries and providing regular updates, they ensured a seamless asset distribution, minimizing misunderstandings and fostering trust. In another instance, an executor managed to avert family conflict by mediating discussions between siblings with differing expectations. By referring back to the detailed guidance provided by the deceased, they were able to uphold the deceased's wishes while addressing each heir's concerns with empathy and transparency. These stories highlight the profound impact of a well-prepared executor, illustrating how thoughtful selection and guidance can preserve family harmony and ensure your estate is administered smoothly.

5.6 Planning for Incapacity: Powers of Attorney and More

Imagine waking up one day unable to make decisions for yourself. It's a sobering thought, yet it highlights the critical importance of planning for potential incapacity. This preparation ensures continuity in your personal and financial affairs, reducing stress for family members who might otherwise struggle with unexpected responsibilities. Without a plan, loved ones are left to guess your wishes, often leading to unnecessary tension and legal hurdles. By addressing these concerns ahead of time, you provide clarity and direction, allowing for a smoother management of your affairs if you can't make decisions on your own.

A key element in planning for incapacity is the power of attorney. This legal document grants a trusted person the authority to manage your affairs, ensuring that someone can act on your behalf when you're unable to. A durable power of attorney is particularly useful for financial decisions. It allows the appointed individual to handle bank accounts, pay bills, and manage investments, providing financial stability even in your absence. Equally important is the healthcare power of attorney, which designates someone to make medical decisions for you. This person will ensure that your healthcare preferences are respected and followed, making critical choices if you're unable to communicate your wishes.

To prepare comprehensively for incapacity, consider implementing several strategies. Creating a healthcare power of attorney is an effective way to outline your medical preferences in detail. This document specifies the types of medical treatments you do or do not want, such as resuscitation or life support, providing clear guidance to your healthcare proxy and medical team. Appointing healthcare proxies is another essential step, as it involves selecting trusted individuals who will advocate for your medical wishes. Their role is to ensure that your healthcare decisions align with your values, offering peace of mind that you'll receive the care you desire, even if you can't voice it yourself.

Consider the example of a woman who thoughtfully planned for her incapacity. She appointed her sister as her durable power of attorney for financial matters and her best friend as her healthcare proxy. When a sudden illness left her unable to make decisions, both appointees stepped in seamlessly, managing her affairs according to her wishes. Her finances remained stable, and her medical care was administered exactly as she had specified in her healthcare power of attorney. This foresight not only ensured her wishes were honored but also relieved her family of the burden of making difficult decisions during a stressful time.

In another scenario, a man who suffered a debilitating stroke had the foresight to have a power of attorney in place. His son, who was appointed to handle financial matters, was able to immediately access bank accounts and pay bills, preventing financial disruption. Meanwhile, his daughter, acting as his healthcare proxy, ensured that his medical treatment followed the instructions laid out in his healthcare power of attorney. This arrangement allowed the family to focus on his recovery rather than being mired in administrative issues, illustrating the profound impact of effective incapacity planning.

These stories highlight the importance of having powers of attorney and healthcare proxies in place. Such planning not only provides a clear path for managing your affairs but also offers reassurance that your wishes will be respected. As you consider your own plan, reflect on who you trust to make decisions on your behalf and ensure they understand your preferences. With these tools, you can face the future with confidence, knowing that both your personal and financial matters are secure, even in the face of unexpected challenges.

5.7 Building a Reliable Support Team: Your Estate Planning Allies

Imagine orchestrating a complex symphony without a conductor. Each section plays its part, but without guidance, harmony is elusive. In estate planning, the conductor is your support team, guiding the process to ensure that each component works in concert with the others. A well-rounded team of professionals brings together diverse expertise and perspectives, addressing your legal, financial, and personal needs in a comprehensive manner. This diversity leads to robust strategies, as each professional brings unique insights that can enhance and refine your estate plan. Lawyers ensure legal compliance and precision, while financial advisors manage and grow your wealth. Accountants and financial planners can navigate the intricacies of tax implications, ensuring that your estate's value is preserved for your heirs. Trust officers and tax specialists add another layer of expertise, providing advice on trust management and tax optimization. Together, these professionals form a cohesive unit, each playing a vital role in crafting an estate plan that reflects your wishes and protects your legacy.

Coordination among team members is crucial for effective estate planning. Regular meetings and updates facilitate communication, allowing each professional to stay informed about changes and developments in your estate. This ongoing dialogue ensures that everyone is aligned with your goals and can collaborate effectively. Clear division of responsibilities is also essential, as it prevents overlaps and ensures that each member focuses on their area of expertise. By defining roles and expectations from the outset, you create a streamlined process where everyone knows their part, reducing the likelihood of miscommunication or errors. This clarity is particularly important in complex estates, where the stakes are high, and the margin for error is small. By fostering a collaborative environment, you empower your team to work together, leveraging their collective knowledge and skills to create an estate plan that is both comprehensive and personal.

Successful team collaboration can lead to remarkable outcomes, as evidenced by numerous real-world examples. Consider a family with a multifaceted estate, encompassing diverse assets and business interests. By assembling a team of trusted professionals, they executed a complex estate plan flawlessly. Each team member contributed their expertise, from legal structuring to financial management, ensuring that the estate was administered smoothly and efficiently. The result was a plan that not only met the family's immediate needs but also positioned them for future success. In another instance, a team of professionals engaged in collaborative brainstorming to address a unique challenge in the estate plan. Their innovative approach led to a breakthrough strategy that optimized asset distribution and minimized tax liabilities, showcasing the power of diverse perspectives working in unison.

These stories highlight the transformative potential of a cohesive support team in estate planning. By bringing together professionals with complementary skills and fostering a collaborative environment, you can create an estate plan that is both resilient and responsive to your needs. This synergy not only enhances the effectiveness of your plan but also provides peace of mind, knowing that your legacy is in capable hands. As you consider your estate planning journey, reflect on the importance of building a reliable support team and the value it can bring to your plan. With the right team in place, you can navigate the complexities of estate planning with confidence, knowing that you have the support and guidance needed to protect your legacy for generations to come.

In this chapter, we've explored the importance of assembling a diverse team of professionals to guide your estate planning. By focusing on coordination and collaboration, you ensure that every facet of your plan is meticulously crafted and aligned with your goals. As we transition to the next chapter, consider how these principles can be applied to other aspects of your estate planning process.

Don't move on to the next chapter without doing the following;

1. Come up with a list of questions you would like to ask your estate lawyer. Don't forget that there's no such thing as a dumb question

2. Do you have a lawyer in mind? Ask friends, family or colleagues for recommendations. Try www.bestlawyers.com and find a recommendation under trusts & estates in your state

3. Meet with 2-3 lawyers and see who you have a rapport with and who you think will do a good job. Don't feel the need to say yes on the spot, let them know you'll come back to them and discuss with your spouse and sleep on the decision overnight

4. Choose a lawyer and draft a trust/will, power of attorney, healthcare power of attorney and healthcare directive as a minimum

5. Can your lawyer cover the tax implications of your estate? If not look for a certified financial planner at www.letsmakeaplan.org where you can search for someone within your state

Chapter 6

Special Considerations and Advanced Strategies

Imagine being able to extend your values and impact well beyond your lifetime, leaving a lasting legacy that reflects not just your financial success but your personal beliefs and aspirations. By weaving charitable giving into your estate planning, you can achieve this and more. Charitable contributions not only provide profound satisfaction and the opportunity to support causes close to your heart, but they also offer significant tax benefits that can enhance your estate's efficiency. This chapter explores how philanthropy can become a cornerstone of your estate plan, ensuring that your wealth continues to make a difference long after you are gone.

6.1 Charitable Giving and Estate Planning: Creating a Legacy

Charitable giving can play a pivotal role in estate planning, aligning your financial decisions with your personal values while offering substantial tax advantages. By incorporating charitable contributions into your estate strategy, you can reduce the taxable portion of your estate and potentially lower your income tax liability. One of the most effective vehicles for achieving these goals is a charitable remainder trust (CRT). This irrevocable trust allows you to donate assets to charity while receiving annual income derived from those assets. The trust pays income to you or other beneficiaries for a term of up to 20 years or for the life of the beneficiaries, after which the remaining assets go to a designated charity. This not only provides a predictable income stream but also defers taxes on asset sales and qualifies you for a partial charitable deduction based on the value of the charitable remainder interest. Another compelling option is the creation of donor-advised funds, which enable you to make a charitable contribution, receive an immediate tax deduction, and then recommend grants from the fund to your favorite charities over time.

There are various methods to integrate philanthropy into your estate plan, each tailored to different goals and levels of involvement. Direct gifts to charities from your estate can be a straightforward approach, allowing specific sums or assets to be transferred to charitable organizations upon your passing. This method can reduce estate taxes, as these gifts are deducted from the taxable estate. Alternatively, setting up a private family foundation can provide a more structured approach, offering the opportunity for your family to be actively involved in philanthropic efforts. Family foundations can support a wide range of initiatives, from education and health to community development, fostering a culture of giving that can be passed down through generations. This approach not only ensures targeted charitable efforts but also involves family members in decision-making processes, strengthening family bonds through shared values and goals.

The tax benefits of charitable contributions are significant and multifaceted. Charitable donations can provide income tax deductions, reducing your taxable income and potentially placing you in a lower tax bracket. Moreover, charitable bequests can lead to estate tax reductions, as the value of the donation is deducted from the taxable estate. This can be particularly advantageous for high-net-worth individuals, for whom estate taxes represent a substantial liability. By strategically planning charitable contributions, you can enhance the efficiency of your estate plan, maximizing the value of your legacy while supporting causes that matter to you.

Consider the story of a family that established a foundation to support underprivileged youth in their community. Through the foundation, they not only provided scholarships and educational resources but also inspired other community members to contribute, amplifying their impact. This initiative not only reflected their commitment to education and equality but also brought their family closer together, as they worked collectively to achieve a common goal. In another example, an individual used a charitable remainder trust to secure lifetime income while planning a substantial gift to a local hospital, ensuring continued support for healthcare services in their area. These narratives illustrate how thoughtful charitable planning can create lasting legacies that extend far beyond financial contributions, touching lives and fostering positive change.

Ensure that this is communicated to your heirs as you don't want them to assume they're inheriting your whole estate, only to find out you're giving some of it away. It's your estate and your choice, but open communication can ensure this is not an issue.

Reflection Section

Reflect on the causes and organizations that resonate most with you. Consider how integrating charitable giving into your estate plan could align with your values and create a meaningful legacy. Jot down a few ideas and think about the impact you'd like to have, both now and in the future. This exercise can help you clarify your philanthropic goals and identify the best strategies to incorporate them into your estate planning.

6.2 Leveraging Tax Havens: Legal Considerations

Imagine the concept of a tax haven as a financial refuge where your estate can breathe a little easier. Essentially, tax havens are jurisdictions that offer favorable tax conditions, enticing individuals and businesses to place their assets there. These havens often feature low or zero tax rates on certain types of income or capital gains, which can significantly reduce the tax burden on your estate. Offshore accounts and trusts are common tools used within these jurisdictions to manage and protect wealth. Establishing a trust in a tax haven can help in ensuring that more of your estate is preserved for your heirs, rather than being consumed by taxes.

With the allure of tax savings, however, comes the necessity of navigating a complex legal landscape. Adhering to international tax laws is paramount to avoid crossing the line from legal tax avoidance to illegal tax evasion. It's crucial to maintain transparency and integrity in all financial dealings, ensuring compliance with both the laws of the tax haven and your home country. This means being meticulous about documentation, reporting all income accurately, and avoiding any activities that could be perceived as deceptive or fraudulent. The ethical considerations are equally important, as the use of tax havens is often scrutinized for potential abuses. Maintaining ethical standards not only protects your legal standing but also upholds your reputation.

Incorporating tax havens into your estate plan requires a strategic approach. Offshore asset protection trusts can be established to shield assets from creditors and legal claims while benefiting from the tax advantages of the host jurisdiction. These trusts are particularly useful in protecting assets from potential litigation or business risks. Another method involves using international business corporations to hold and manage assets. This structure can provide operational flexibility and tax efficiency, especially for those with business interests in multiple countries. It's essential, though, to work with legal and financial experts who specialize in international tax law to ensure that your strategies are both effective and compliant. For the majority of us, this type of complex planning will not be of interest but for those who might have a complex asset base, this can be one of your lawyer interview questions.

Consider the case of an estate that successfully leveraged Switzerland-based trusts to preserve wealth. Switzerland's reputation for financial privacy and favorable tax laws made it an ideal location for establishing trusts that protected the estate's value. By carefully structuring the trusts and complying with Swiss regulations, the estate managed to shield its assets from excessive taxation, benefiting the beneficiaries significantly. In another scenario, an individual used Cayman Islands accounts to reduce tax liabilities. The Cayman Islands, known for their business-friendly tax policies, provided the perfect environment to manage investments without the heavy burden of taxes. These examples illustrate how, with careful planning and adherence to legal standards, tax havens can be a valuable component of an estate plan, offering both protection and efficiency.

6.3 Navigating International Estates: Cross-Border Planning

As our world becomes increasingly interconnected, the complexities of managing an estate that spans multiple countries are more common than ever. Many families find themselves balancing assets and heirs across diverse legal landscapes. Each country brings its own legal systems and tax codes, which can create a labyrinth of regulations that must be navigated carefully. For instance, an asset located in one country might be subject to entirely different tax obligations than an asset held domestically. Moreover, the fluctuating nature of currency exchange rates adds another layer of complexity, impacting the value of assets and creating potential financial uncertainties. This can make planning an international estate both challenging and intricate, as you must account for the potential for both immediate and long-term fluctuations in asset value.

Successfully managing an international estate requires a strategic approach that anticipates these challenges. One effective method is to leverage bilateral treaties and international agreements that can simplify tax obligations and clarify legal requirements. These treaties often provide mechanisms for avoiding double taxation, ensuring that your estate isn't taxed by both countries involved. Another strategy is the creation of dual wills, which allow for separate wills to govern assets located in different jurisdictions. This approach can streamline the legal process, ensuring that your wishes are respected in each country without conflicting legal interpretations. These wills must be carefully drafted to avoid contradictions and ensure that each aligns with the legal requirements of the respective jurisdictions.

The intricacies of international estate planning underscore the vital role of experienced professionals. Retaining a lawyer specializing in international law is crucial, as they can navigate the nuances of cross-border regulations and ensure compliance with all relevant legal codes. These experts can illuminate the intricacies of jurisdictional laws, helping to mitigate potential conflicts and ensure that your estate plan is executed smoothly. Collaborating with global financial advisors is equally important, as they can provide insights into managing currency exchange risks and optimizing the financial aspects of your estate. Their expertise can be invaluable in structuring your estate to minimize tax liabilities and protect your assets from legal entanglements.

Consider the story of an individual who successfully navigated the complexities of an estate spanning the United States and several European countries. This person employed a team of international legal experts and financial advisors to craft a plan that respected both U.S. and EU inheritance laws. By utilizing bilateral treaties, they were able to prevent double taxation, preserving more of the estate for the heirs. In another case, a business owner with interests in Asia and Europe managed global operations through international trusts. This allowed them to maintain control and ensure that the business continued to thrive across borders, while also protecting their assets from potential legal challenges. These examples highlight how strategic planning and professional expertise can turn the complexities of international estates into manageable undertakings.

6.4 Using Life Insurance in Estate Planning

Life insurance can serve as a cornerstone in estate planning, playing a pivotal role in meeting diverse goals that ensure both peace of mind and financial security. One of the primary benefits of life insurance is its ability to provide liquidity for estate taxes. When an estate is subject to taxes, having immediate cash on hand can prevent the sale of valuable assets that you'd rather preserve within the family. Life insurance proceeds, being generally tax-free, can cover these obligations seamlessly, ensuring your heirs are not burdened with finding quick solutions under stressful circumstances. Additionally, life insurance can guarantee financial support for dependents, offering a safety net that maintains their standard of living. This assurance is crucial for families with young children or for those relying on a single income, providing stability in uncertain times.

Different types of life insurance policies cater to varied needs and financial strategies within your estate plan. Whole life insurance offers lifelong coverage with a savings component, accumulating cash value over time, which can be borrowed against if needed. This makes it an attractive option for those looking to build wealth steadily while ensuring continuous protection. Conversely, term life insurance provides coverage for a specific period, usually at a lower cost, making it ideal for temporary needs like mortgage protection or supporting children through college. Universal life insurance stands out for its flexibility, combining permanent coverage with the potential for wealth accumulation. This type allows you to adjust premiums and death benefits as your financial situation evolves, offering a dynamic tool that adapts to your changing needs.

Maximizing the benefits of life insurance requires strategic planning and the use of advanced tactics. One such strategy involves the establishment of an irrevocable life insurance trust (ILIT). By placing a life insurance policy within an ILIT, you remove the policy's proceeds from your taxable estate, potentially saving a significant amount in estate taxes. This trust not only protects insurance benefits from creditors but also ensures that proceeds are distributed according to your specific wishes, whether that's to fund education, support a surviving spouse, or equalize inheritances among heirs. Equalizing inheritances can be particularly valuable in blended families or when certain heirs receive tangible assets, like a family home or business, while others might receive liquid assets.

Consider the story of a family whose patriarch used life insurance to address estate taxes effectively. By taking out a policy with a substantial death benefit and placing it in an ILIT, he ensured that the estate taxes were covered without liquidating family properties that held sentimental value. The insurance payout provided the necessary liquidity, preserving the family's legacy intact. In another scenario, a single parent utilized life insurance to secure their children's future. The policy was designed to provide a structured financial support system, ensuring that the children would have the means for education and daily living, regardless of unforeseen circumstances. This foresight offered reassurance that the children would be cared for, maintaining the lifestyle and opportunities envisioned by the parent.

These examples highlight the strategic use of life insurance in estate planning, showing how it can address both immediate financial challenges and long-term goals. By understanding the different types of policies available and employing strategies like ILITs, you can craft a plan that not only meets your obligations but also supports your broader aspirations, ensuring that your legacy is protected and your family is provided for. As you consider incorporating life insurance into your estate plan, reflect on your specific needs, family dynamics, and financial objectives to determine the best path forward.

6.5 Asset Protection Trusts: Shielding Your Wealth

Imagine a fortress surrounding your most valuable assets, protecting them from unforeseen threats. Asset protection trusts serve much like this fortress, providing a legal structure that safeguards your wealth from creditors and potential legal claims. At their core, these trusts are designed to ensure that your assets remain within your control, free from the reach of those who might seek to claim them. By placing your assets in an asset protection trust, you shield them from financial predators, allowing you to manage and distribute them as you see fit. This not only offers peace of mind but also ensures that your resources are preserved for future generations, aligned with your wishes.

Creating and managing an asset protection trust requires careful planning and a strategic approach. Selecting the appropriate jurisdiction is a crucial first step. Some regions offer more favorable legal environments for asset protection, such as the Cook Islands or Nevis, known for their robust trust laws that favor settlors. Choosing the right jurisdiction can significantly impact the effectiveness of your trust, offering enhanced protection against legal claims. Equally important is the appointment of a trustworthy trustee who will oversee the trust's operations. This individual or entity should possess integrity and financial acumen, as they will be responsible for managing the assets and executing the terms of the trust. It's vital to establish clear guidelines and communicate your expectations to ensure the trustee acts in alignment with your goals.

Legal considerations and limitations play a pivotal role in the establishment and maintenance of asset protection trusts. Understanding fraudulent conveyance laws is crucial, as these laws prevent individuals from transferring assets into a trust with the intent to defraud creditors. Any attempt to hide assets from legitimate claims can lead to legal challenges and the potential invalidation of the trust. Maintaining transparency with legal requirements is therefore essential, ensuring that all actions comply with applicable laws and regulations. This transparency not only upholds the trust's integrity but also protects you from legal repercussions, preserving the trust's effectiveness as a shield.

Consider the story of a business owner who used an asset protection trust to safeguard personal wealth from potential litigation. Facing uncertain economic conditions, this individual sought to protect their assets from creditors while maintaining control over their distribution. By establishing the trust in a jurisdiction with strong protective laws and appointing a skilled trustee, they successfully insulated their assets from external claims. This strategy provided the owner with financial security, allowing them to focus on business growth without the constant worry of asset exposure. In another instance, a family protected their estate from a contentious legal battle by placing key assets in an asset protection trust. This move not only preserved the family's wealth but also ensured that the assets were distributed according to the family's wishes, free from external interference. These examples underscore the value of asset protection trusts in providing a secure environment for your wealth, enabling you to manage and preserve it with confidence.

In this chapter, we've covered the more complex estate planning scenarios. Don't be too concerned if these are confusing even after reading the information, as for most people this complexity won't be necessary. I've included it more for information and for you to ask your lawyer if it applies to you. A standard will/trust, power of attorney and healthcare directive should suffice for most people.

Don't move on to the next chapter without doing the following;

1. Do you want to incorporate charitable giving into your estate plan? Ensure you communicate this to your estate lawyer so they can create the appropriate structure to do this in

2. Do you have a more complex, international asset base? Prepare questions for your lawyer about the ideal way to handle this complexity

3. Do you have life insurance policies? Ask your lawyer if they are structured to your estate's advantage. If not you may need to change the structure to benefit your heirs and reduce the tax burden

Chapter 7

Real-Life Examples and Case Studies

Life often throws unexpected challenges our way, and when it comes to estate planning, these challenges can seem daunting. Consider the story of the Thompsons, a typical middle-aged family striving to secure their future amidst the bustle of everyday life. With both parents in their 40s, they found themselves caught between demanding careers and the pressing need to plan for their teenage children's future. Like many families, they initially hesitated to confront the realities of estate planning, finding it difficult to carve out time for conversations about mortality.

The Thompsons' journey began with the realization that their current lack of a formal plan left them vulnerable. They recognized the importance of establishing wills and healthcare directives to ensure their wishes were honored. This meant finding time to meet with advisors, a task complicated by their hectic schedules. Balancing work obligations with the need to address these personal matters required careful planning and a commitment to prioritize these discussions. By setting aside dedicated time to meet with estate planning professionals, they were able to outline a comprehensive plan that provided a clear road map for the future.

One of the key steps the Thompsons took was setting up education funds and trusts for their children. This decision was driven by their desire to secure their children's education, ensuring that financial resources would be available regardless of unforeseen circumstances. By establishing these trusts, they provided a structured way to manage and allocate funds specifically for educational purposes. This foresight not only guaranteed that their children's educational needs would be met but also offered peace of mind, knowing that these resources were protected and available when needed.

Initially, the Thompsons faced several obstacles. The most significant challenge was overcoming their initial reluctance to discuss topics related to mortality. Like many, they found it uncomfortable to contemplate their own passing and the impact it would have on their family. However, by acknowledging these feelings and engaging in open dialogue, they were able to confront their apprehensions and move forward with a sense of purpose. Another hurdle was managing their complex schedules to accommodate meetings with advisors. To address this, they worked collaboratively, coordinating their calendars and setting appointments well in advance to ensure they stayed on track. Today with the ease of online appointments, this should be a lot easier with most lawyers offering online consultations.

The outcomes of the Thompsons' planning efforts were transformative. With established wills and healthcare directives, they achieved a level of financial security that provided them with peace of mind. They knew that their assets would be distributed according to their wishes and that their children's future was safeguarded. The creation of education trusts ensured that their children's academic aspirations were supported, offering them opportunities without financial constraints. This comprehensive approach to estate planning allowed the Thompsons to focus on the present, knowing that they had taken proactive steps to protect their family's future.

Reflection Section

Reflect on your current estate planning situation. Consider the priorities you have for your family's future and how a comprehensive estate plan could address these needs. Write down any concerns or goals you have regarding asset distribution, healthcare directives, or education funds. Use this reflection as a foundation to begin or update your own estate planning process, ensuring it aligns with your values and aspirations.

7.1 Case Study: Retirees Finalizing Their Legacies

Meet John and Linda, a couple in their late 60s, who found themselves at a pivotal moment in life. With the echoes of a bustling career life growing fainter, they turned their focus toward finalizing their estate plans. Their primary goal was to preserve their legacy and ensure that their assets would be distributed in a way that reflected their life's work and values. They were particularly keen on minimizing the tax burden for their heirs, allowing their children to benefit fully from the wealth they had accumulated over decades. John and Linda knew that the key to achieving these objectives lay in meticulous planning and strategic action.

To address their goals, the couple decided to establish a living trust. This decision was pivotal. By moving their assets into the trust, John and Linda could manage their estate effectively while avoiding the often lengthy and costly probate process. A living trust also provided them with the flexibility to make adjustments as their circumstances changed, a feature they found reassuring. Additionally, they employed gifting strategies to reduce their taxable estate. By gifting a portion of their wealth to their children while they were still alive, they could decrease the size of their estate, thus minimizing potential estate taxes. This strategy not only benefited their heirs financially but also allowed John and Linda to witness the positive impact of their generosity firsthand.

Navigating complex tax regulations was one of the significant challenges John and Linda faced. The intricacies of tax law can be daunting, and the couple knew they needed expert guidance. They worked closely with a financial advisor who specialized in estate planning, ensuring that they had a clear understanding of the implications of each decision. This collaboration proved invaluable, providing them with peace of mind that their plans were both legally sound and tax-efficient. Another hurdle was ensuring clear communication with family members. Open conversations about estate planning can be uncomfortable, but John and Linda were determined to avoid misunderstandings. They organized family meetings to discuss their plans, explaining their decisions and addressing any concerns. This transparency helped to foster trust and understanding, ensuring that their intentions were clear to all involved.

The legacy John and Linda left behind was marked by harmony and generosity. Their thoughtful planning ensured that their family experienced a smooth transition, with clear instructions that left no room for disputes. The equitable distribution of assets reflected their commitment to fairness, providing each heir with a sense of security and respect. Moreover, John and Linda's charitable contributions had a lasting impact on their community. They chose to support several local projects, from educational initiatives to community health programs, aligning their legacy with causes they cared deeply about. These contributions not only enriched the community but also inspired their family to continue this tradition of giving, creating a ripple effect of positive change.

Their story illustrates how thoughtful estate planning can shape the future not just for family, but for the broader community. The legacy of John and Linda serves as a testament to the power of strategic planning and open communication, showing that with the right approach, the complexities of estate planning can be transformed into a clear and meaningful path forward.

7.2 Case Study: High-Net-Worth Individuals Preserving Wealth

In the fast-paced world of technology, where innovation is the currency of success, the founders of a thriving tech company stood at a crossroads. As high-net-worth individuals, their focus extended beyond the immediate growth of their business to the broader horizon of preserving their wealth for the future. With significant real estate holdings and a diverse investment portfolio, they faced the intricate task of ensuring their financial legacy would endure across generations. Their enterprise, a beacon of their hard work and vision, had grown exponentially, and with it came the responsibility of safeguarding their assets against the unpredictable tides of the economic landscape.

To address these challenges, they turned to advanced estate planning strategies, employing sophisticated tools and techniques that matched the complexity of their circumstances. One of their primary actions was creating asset protection trusts. These trusts served as a shield, safeguarding their wealth from potential creditors and unforeseen liabilities. By strategically placing assets within these trusts, they could mitigate risks and maintain control over their distribution. This approach not only protected their financial interests but also ensured that their wealth could be transferred smoothly to future generations without the encumbrance of legal disputes.

In addition to asset protection trusts, they implemented key person insurance to fortify their business continuity plan. This insurance was a crucial component, providing financial security in the unfortunate event of losing a pivotal team member. It ensured that the business could weather the storm of such a loss without compromising its operational stability. By securing key person insurance, they reinforced their commitment to the company's longevity, minimizing disruption and safeguarding the livelihoods of their employees. This strategic foresight allowed them to maintain the confidence of investors and stakeholders, essential for a company that thrived on innovation and trust.

The path was not without its complexities. Balancing their business interests with personal wealth management required a delicate touch. They navigated the intricate landscape of compliance with evolving tax laws, a task that demanded constant vigilance and expert guidance. The dynamic nature of tax legislation meant they had to stay informed and adaptable, ensuring their strategies remained effective and compliant. Collaborating with seasoned tax advisors, they crafted a plan that aligned with the latest regulations, optimizing their tax efficiency while preserving their wealth.

The outcomes of their meticulous planning were profound. Their wealth, carefully preserved through astute management, stood as a testament to their foresight and strategic acumen. Across generations, their family benefited from the infrastructure they had established, enjoying financial security and opportunities to pursue their passions. The business, under new leadership, continued to thrive, fueled by the solid foundation they had laid. This transition, seamless and harmonious, reflected their commitment to nurturing the next wave of innovation and leadership within the company. Their legacy, built on a foundation of strategic planning and thoughtful stewardship, inspired confidence and set a standard for future generations to emulate.

7.3 Case Study: Parents Securing Their Children's Futures

Meet Sarah and David, young parents with two energetic toddlers, deeply committed to ensuring their children's welfare through estate planning. Like many parents, they were initially overwhelmed by the myriad of decisions that estate planning requires, but their primary concern was clear: Who would care for their children if they were no longer around? This question, daunting as it is, propelled them into action. They realized that without a plan, their children's future could be left to chance, and they wanted to ensure that their kids would be raised in an environment that mirrored their own values and aspirations.

Their first step was to appoint guardians, a decision fraught with emotional complexity. Choosing who would raise their children in their absence was no small feat. They considered family members and close friends, weighing factors such as parenting styles, financial stability, and the ability to provide a nurturing home. After much deliberation, they selected David's sister and her husband, a couple they trusted implicitly and who shared similar values. To formalize this decision, they included a guardianship clause in their wills, ensuring that their wishes were legally binding.

In tandem with appointing guardians, Sarah and David established trusts to secure their children's financial future. They were determined to provide for their children's education and general welfare, no matter what life had in store. By setting up these trusts, they could designate funds specifically for their children's needs, safeguarding these resources from potential misuse. In addition, they purchased life insurance policies to replace their income in the event of an untimely death. This step was crucial, as it ensured that financial burdens would not fall on the guardians, allowing them to focus on raising the children with love and stability.

The journey wasn't without its challenges. Sarah and David initially struggled with the decision of who should serve as guardians. The weight of this choice was heavy, knowing it would shape their children's lives profoundly. They also faced the daunting task of balancing immediate financial needs with long-term planning. Prioritizing current expenses while setting aside funds for future security required careful budgeting and a clear understanding of their financial landscape. They tackled these challenges by engaging in open discussions with their chosen guardians, ensuring everyone was on the same page regarding expectations and responsibilities.

The benefits of their careful planning soon became evident. With guardian-ship legally established, Sarah and David had peace of mind, knowing that their children would be cared for by people they trusted. The trusts they set up provided a stable financial foundation, assuring that their children's education and well-being were protected. The life insurance policies further enhanced this security, offering a financial safety net that allowed David's sister and her husband to focus on providing emotional support and stability rather than worrying about financial constraints.

Sarah and David's story highlights the profound impact that thoughtful estate planning can have on a family. By taking proactive steps, they ensured that their children would be cared for and supported, no matter what the future held. This foresight not only protected their children's futures but also granted Sarah and David the peace of mind to enjoy their time with their kids, knowing they had taken every possible step to secure their well-being.

7.4 Case Study: Blended Families Achieving Equitable Distribution

Imagine a family where love has woven together two distinct histories into one vibrant tapestry. Meet the Johnsons, a blended family navigating the complexities of equitable asset distribution. Both parents entered this union with children from previous marriages, each carrying unique expectations and emotional ties to their past. The challenge was clear: how to distribute assets in a way that honors these diverse familial and financial dynamics while maintaining harmony within the family.

In tackling this intricate landscape, the Johnsons adopted a thoughtful approach to estate planning. They began by establishing separate trusts for each set of the biological children. This strategy allowed them to allocate resources in a manner that respected the individual needs of each child, ensuring that no one felt overlooked or undervalued. By clearly defining the terms of these trusts, they provided a structured framework for asset distribution that reflected their shared values and commitment to fairness. This separation also offered protection, as it guaranteed that each child would receive their intended inheritance without the risk of disputes.

Central to their planning process were regular family meetings, where they openly discussed inheritance plans and expectations. These gatherings became a cornerstone of their approach, providing a platform for each family member to voice their thoughts and concerns. Through these discussions, the Johnsons fostered an environment of transparency and understanding, addressing potential conflicts before they could escalate. This open communication was vital in managing differing expectations and emotions, which naturally arise in blended families. By acknowledging and respecting each person's perspective, they were able to build a consensus that honored their collective bond.

Despite their proactive efforts, the Johnsons faced inevitable challenges. Differing expectations among family members posed a significant hurdle. Children accustomed to certain traditions or lifestyles from their previous family experiences had to adjust to new norms and financial realities. The parents recognized these emotional complexities and worked diligently to ensure that each child felt heard and included in the process. Clear communication was their most powerful tool, as it helped to bridge gaps and align their diverse perspectives. By maintaining a focus on shared values and goals, they navigated these emotional waters with empathy and patience.

The outcomes of the Johnsons' meticulous planning were remarkable. Through transparent and fair asset division, they achieved a level of harmony that many might find elusive in blended families. Each child understood their place within the family structure and felt secure in the knowledge that their needs and desires had been considered. This equitable distribution not only preserved family unity but also strengthened the bonds between siblings from different marriages. The Johnsons' story illustrates how thoughtful estate planning can transform potential conflict into an opportunity for deeper connection and mutual respect.

In this case, the Johnsons demonstrated that with careful planning and open dialogue, blended families can navigate the complexities of asset distribution successfully. Their story serves as a testament to the power of transparency and fairness in estate planning, offering a road map for other families facing similar challenges. Through their efforts, they not only secured their financial legacy but also fortified the emotional foundation of their family, ensuring that it would thrive for generations to come.

7.5 Lessons Learned from Common Mistakes in Estate Planning

Estate planning is a critical task rife with potential pitfalls. One of the most common mistakes people make is failing to update their plans after significant life changes. Imagine a scenario where a parent drafts a will in their 30s, yet never revisits it as decades pass. Children are born, relationships change, and assets grow, yet the will remains a relic of the past. This oversight can lead to unintended heirs receiving assets or, worse, loved ones being excluded altogether. It's a stark reminder of the necessity of regular reviews, which ensure that your plans evolve alongside your life circumstances. Regular updates are not just prudent but essential to reflect the dynamic nature of life.

In today's digital age, another frequent oversight is underestimating the complexity of digital assets. Many of us have a vast array of online accounts, from social media to digital wallets, which can hold significant financial and sentimental value. Yet, these assets often go unmentioned in traditional estate plans. Without proper documentation, these digital treasures may be inaccessible to heirs, effectively lost in the ether. This oversight leaves a gap in your legacy, as cherished memories and valuable assets remain locked away, beyond the reach of your family. Recognizing the importance of including digital assets in your estate plan is crucial to ensure a comprehensive approach.

Real-life examples illustrate the repercussions of these mistakes. Take the case of an outdated will that resulted in unintended heirs benefiting from an estate. This family faced a legal quagmire, as distant relatives contested the distribution, leading to a lengthy and costly court battle. The emotional toll was significant, with family members grappling with feelings of betrayal and confusion. Similarly, another family encountered disputes due to unclear asset distribution. The lack of a clear directive led to fractured relationships, as siblings argued over what they believed their parents had intended. These scenarios highlight the importance of clarity and foresight in estate planning, underscoring the need for meticulous documentation and communication.

Addressing these errors involves strategic action. Estate plans must be revised to reflect current circumstances, ensuring that they align with your present reality and future aspirations. This means setting a schedule for regular reviews, perhaps annually or after major life events, to keep your plans relevant. Additionally, mediation can be a valuable tool in resolving family conflicts. Bringing in a neutral party to facilitate discussions can help clarify intentions and rebuild trust, turning potential discord into an opportunity for growth. By tackling these issues head-on, you can transform a potentially divisive process into one that strengthens familial bonds.

The key takeaways for readers are clear. Regular plan reviews and updates are vital to maintaining the integrity and accuracy of your estate documents. A comprehensive plan should include all assets, tangible and digital, to ensure nothing is left to chance. Communication is also critical; discussing your plans with family members can prevent surprises and misunderstandings, fostering an environment of transparency and trust. By learning from these lessons, you can navigate the complexities of estate planning with confidence, securing your legacy for generations to come.

In reflecting on these lessons, we see how estate planning is not just a legal exercise, but a deeply personal one. It requires us to confront our own mortality and consider the legacy we wish to leave behind. By avoiding common mistakes and taking proactive steps, you can create a plan that not only protects your assets but also honors your values and relationships. The insights gained from these experiences pave the way for a more thoughtful and intentional approach to estate planning, ensuring that your wishes are fulfilled and your loved ones are cared for.

In this chapter, some of the examples will reflect your family situation. Take these examples as ideas or questions you can take to your initial meeting with your lawyer to ask questions or include in your will/trust.

Don't move on to the next chapter without doing the following;

1. Do you want specific clauses in your will/trust regarding education wishes? Add this to your list to inform your lawyer when drafting your will/trust

2. Was there anything in these examples that prompted you to ask questions of your lawyer that you might add to your will/trust? Make sure to jot these down

Chapter 8

Maintaining and Updating Your Estate Plan

Imagine a garden filled with carefully chosen plants, thriving under the sun. Like a garden, your estate plan requires regular attention and care to ensure it continues to flourish. Over time, as seasons change, so do your life circumstances. Just like tending to that garden, updating your estate plan doesn't just maintain its beauty; it protects its very existence. Life is unpredictable, and several key events demand that you revisit and revise your estate plan to reflect your current wishes and responsibilities. Ignoring these changes can lead to unintended consequences, leaving your loved ones with confusion and potential disputes.

8.1 Life Changes and Estate Planning: When to Update

Marriage and divorce are significant life milestones that necessitate a re-evaluation of your estate plan. When you marry, your financial and legal obligations shift, and you may wish to include your spouse as a beneficiary or appoint them to a decision-making role in case of incapacitation. Conversely, divorce is a time to reassess your beneficiaries and executors. Failing to remove an ex-spouse from your will or trust could result in them inheriting assets you no longer wish them to have, creating a scenario that could be both emotionally and financially problematic.

The arrival of a new child, whether by birth or adoption, is another pivotal moment that warrants immediate attention to your estate plan. This joyous occasion brings with it the responsibility to ensure your child is provided for, both financially and legally. Adding your new child as a beneficiary and appointing a guardian in the event of your untimely death are crucial steps. Without these updates, your child might not receive the benefits you intended or, worse, be left without a clear plan for their care.

Financial changes, such as a significant increase or decrease in wealth, should prompt a thorough review and update of your estate plan. Perhaps you've received a substantial inheritance or acquired valuable assets. These changes impact the distribution of your estate and may necessitate new tax strategies or adjustments to existing ones. On the other hand, financial setbacks might require you to reconsider how much you can afford to leave to beneficiaries or to charitable causes.

Even something as seemingly mundane as overseas travel can trigger the need for an estate plan update. Extended travel or relocation abroad introduces new legal and logistical considerations, such as appointing a temporary power of attorney or updating healthcare directives to reflect local laws and practices. It's essential to ensure that your estate plan accommodates these changes so that your affairs remain in order, regardless of your location.

Neglecting to update your estate plan can lead to unintended heirs or beneficiaries—people who may no longer be part of your life or whom you never intended to include. Misalignment with your current wishes can create confusion and conflict among family members, leading to disputes that could have been avoided with proactive planning. To prevent such issues, it's wise to set reminders for regular updates and maintain a checklist of potential life changes that might affect your estate plan.

Reflection Section

Checklist for Life Changes:

- Marriage or divorce
- Birth or adoption of a child
- Significant changes in financial status
- Extended overseas travel
- Death of a beneficiary, guardian or executor

Consider reviewing this checklist periodically and setting reminders to revisit your estate plan whenever any of these key events occur. Keeping your estate plan aligned with your life ensures that your wishes are respected and your loved ones are cared for as you intend.

8.2 Conducting an Annual Estate Plan Review

Think of your estate plan as a living document, one that breathes and adapts with the changes in your life. Conducting an annual review of your estate plan isn't just a good practice; it's a necessary one to ensure that your plan aligns with your current wishes and life circumstances. Regular reviews provide the opportunity to address potential issues before they become real problems. By revisiting your estate plan each year, you can verify that your intentions are accurately reflected, and that no detail is overlooked. This proactive approach helps to prevent costly oversights, ensuring that the future you've envisioned for your loved ones remains intact.

To begin an annual estate plan review, start by examining any shifts in your assets or liabilities over the past year. This might include purchasing new property, acquiring stocks, or even selling off assets. Each change can impact the distribution of your estate and may require adjustments to your plan. Next, scrutinize your beneficiary designations. Life changes rapidly, and someone who was once a primary beneficiary may no longer hold that position in your heart or life. Confirm that the beneficiaries listed on accounts like life insurance policies, retirement funds, or payable-on-death accounts still align with your current intentions. Lastly, consider your healthcare directives. These documents should reflect your current preferences and designate someone you trust to make medical decisions if needed. Updating these directives ensures that your medical care aligns with your values and wishes. If you do make changes to your healthcare directives ensure you tell your proxy about these changes.

There are various tools and resources available to streamline your estate plan review. Estate planning software can be particularly useful, offering a centralized platform to track changes and store important documents. These digital solutions often include features like automatic reminders for updates and comprehensive checklists to guide you through the evaluation process. Such tools ensure that you cover every facet of your estate plan, leaving no stone unturned. A checklist, whether digital or printed, can provide a structured approach to your review, helping you stay organized and focused on each essential element.

The benefits of conducting regular reviews are illustrated through the experiences of families who have avoided significant challenges thanks to timely updates. Consider a family who, through annual assessments, identified that their youngest child was not listed as a beneficiary on a significant life insurance policy. By catching this oversight early, they amended their plan to ensure equal provision for all their children. Another family discovered, during their review, that a piece of property they intended to leave to a specific heir had increased in value significantly. Adjusting their estate plan to account for this change helped them avoid future probate complications and ensured a smoother transition of assets.

Such stories highlight the importance of maintaining an estate plan that evolves with you, responding to life's unexpected turns. By dedicating time each year to review your estate plan, you're not just safeguarding your assets; you're ensuring that your legacy reflects the person you've become and the family you cherish. This foresight protects your loved ones from unnecessary legal entanglements and emotional distress, allowing them to focus on celebrating your life and honoring your wishes.

8.3 Keeping Up with Legal Changes: Staying Informed

Imagine the legal landscape as a shifting tide, constantly reshaping the shoreline of estate planning. Changes in tax laws or estate thresholds can dramatically alter the benefits your heirs receive. For instance, a reduction in the estate tax exemption could mean that more of your estate's value is subject to taxation, reducing what your beneficiaries ultimately receive. Similarly, new regulations impacting trusts or wills may require you to adjust existing documents to ensure compliance and effectiveness. Without staying informed, you risk leaving your estate plan vulnerable to these changes, potentially undermining your intentions and creating unnecessary complications for your heirs.

Staying current with legal changes might seem daunting, but there are practical strategies you can employ to keep informed. Subscribing to legal newsletters or updates is a straightforward way to receive the latest information directly to your inbox. These resources often provide insights into new laws or regulations and their implications for estate planning. Additionally, attending estate planning seminars or webinars can offer valuable opportunities to learn from experts and ask questions specific to your situation. These events can also introduce you to new tools and practices that might benefit your estate plan.

Legal advisors play a pivotal role in navigating these changes. Regular consultations with an estate planning lawyer ensure that your plan remains robust and compliant with current laws. These professionals can interpret complex legal language and provide personalized advice on how changes might affect your estate. Relying on their expertise allows you to adjust your plan proactively, rather than reactively, ensuring that your intentions are preserved and your beneficiaries are protected.

Consider a family who, through frequent consultations with their legal advisor, adjusted their estate plan in anticipation of changes to tax laws. Their advisor informed them of an upcoming decrease in the estate tax exemption, prompting them to restructure their assets to minimize tax liabilities. Thanks to this proactive approach, their heirs received the full benefits intended for them, avoiding unexpected tax burdens. Another example involves a business owner who, by staying informed about new regulations affecting trusts, was able to amend their trust documents to maintain control over their business's future. This adjustment ensured that the business could continue operating smoothly, even after the owner's passing, preserving jobs and supporting the community.

These examples underscore the importance of awareness and proactive planning in estate management. By staying informed and engaging with legal advisors, you ensure that your estate plan remains aligned with the ever-changing legal environment. This vigilance protects your legacy and offers peace of mind, knowing that your affairs are in order and your beneficiaries will receive what you intended. As laws evolve, so should your plan, reflecting not only the current legal landscape but also your ongoing commitment to safeguarding your family's future.

8.4 Communicating Your Plan to Family Members

Clear communication about your estate plan is like setting a sturdy foundation for your family's future. It prevents misunderstandings and conflicts that might arise in the absence of clarity. When your loved ones understand their roles and responsibilities, they can act confidently, knowing they are fulfilling your wishes. This transparency ensures that everyone is on the same page, reducing the potential for disputes that often occur when plans are ambiguous or unknown. Imagine the relief your family will feel, knowing exactly what you intended and how to carry out your desires. It's a gift of clarity, allowing them to focus on supporting each other during challenging times without the added burden of guessing your intentions.

Discussing estate plans with your family can be daunting, but there are effective strategies to ease the process. Holding family meetings is a practical approach. These gatherings provide a forum for open dialogue, where you can explain your decisions and answer any questions. These discussions should be documented, serving as a reference for future review. This helps to memorialize the conversation, reducing the likelihood of misinterpretations later on. Such documentation can be invaluable, especially if family dynamics change over time or if memories of the discussion fade. It's a proactive way to ensure everyone remembers the agreed-upon plan, enhancing the sense of security and understanding.

Challenges can arise when discussing estate plans, often stemming from emotional reactions to sensitive topics. Talking about death and inheritance can stir deep-seated feelings, making some family members uncomfortable or defensive. Managing these emotions requires patience and empathy. It's important to listen actively and acknowledge everyone's feelings, even if they differ from your own. Balancing transparency with privacy concerns is another hurdle. While it's crucial to be open about your plans, you may not wish to disclose every detail to every family member. Finding the right balance ensures that those who need to know are informed, while still respecting your privacy.

Consider a family who regularly convenes to discuss their estate plan. By fostering an environment of openness and trust, they have achieved consensus on key decisions, such as guardianship for younger children and the management of shared assets. This regular communication has strengthened their bonds, as each member feels valued and heard. In another example, a family successfully avoided disputes by clearly outlining their expectations in a series of documented meetings. By addressing potential concerns upfront and providing space for questions, they ensured that everyone understood their roles and responsibilities. These examples highlight the power of communication in creating harmony and reducing conflict within families.

Effective communication about your estate plan is not just about sharing information; it's about building trust and ensuring your loved ones are prepared to honor your wishes. By engaging openly and honestly, you can create a legacy of understanding and cooperation that transcends mere financial considerations. This foundation of trust and clarity allows your family to move forward with confidence, united in purpose and intent.

8.5 Digital Tools and Resources for Ongoing Management

In today's fast-paced world, technology is an invaluable ally in managing and updating your estate plan. Online platforms have transformed the way we handle our estate documents, offering a digital haven for secure review and storage. Imagine having all your essential documents organized and accessible at the click of a button. These platforms provide a centralized location where you can safely store your will, trusts, and other important documents, making it easier for you—and your designated executors—to locate and access them when needed. Additionally, apps designed for tracking asset changes and plan updates can be a game-changer like You Need a Budget and Mint. They allow you to monitor shifts in your financial landscape, ensuring that your estate plan remains current and reflective of your true intentions.

Security is paramount when dealing with sensitive information, and digital tools offer robust features to keep your data safe. Look for platforms that use data encryption to protect your documents from unauthorized access. This ensures that only those with permission can view or modify your estate plan. Secure access protocols, such as two-factor authentication, add an extra layer of protection by requiring additional verification to gain entry. Moreover, regular software updates are critical as they address potential vulnerabilities and enhance functionality, keeping your digital estate management tools reliable and effective. Backing up your data is another essential practice, as it safeguards your information against loss due to technical failures or human error.

The effectiveness of digital management is best illustrated through real-world examples. Consider the executor who, thanks to a secure online portal, could access the deceased's estate plan effortlessly, eliminating the need for time-consuming searches through physical files. This streamlined access not only sped up the probate process but also reduced stress for the family. Another scenario involves a business owner who used an app to keep track of asset inventories in real-time. This allowed for immediate updates to their estate plan following any significant financial transactions, ensuring that their plan was always in sync with their current financial status.

When selecting the right digital tools, it's important to evaluate software based on its features and ease of use. User-friendly interfaces make it easier to navigate and manage your estate plan, even for those who may not be tech-savvy. Most people have heard of and use Dropbox which has encryption and is cloud-based. Consider whether the software can integrate with existing financial apps you already use, as this can provide a more cohesive view of your financial situation. For instance, integration with budgeting or investment apps can offer insights into asset changes that might necessitate updates to your estate plan. By choosing tools that align with your needs and lifestyle, you can simplify the management of your estate, ensuring that it remains a true reflection of your wishes and circumstances.

8.6 Creating a Legacy Beyond Financial Planning

Legacy planning transcends the simple distribution of wealth, shaping how you're remembered and the values you impart to future generations. It's about passing on not just assets, but also life lessons and cherished memories. Consider supporting charitable causes or community projects that resonate with your values. Establishing scholarships or educational funds in your name can provide lasting opportunities for others, reflecting your commitment to education and personal growth. Documenting and sharing your family history and traditions is another powerful way to create a meaningful legacy. These stories and customs serve as a bridge between generations, helping your loved ones understand where they come from and the values you hold dear.

Engaging your family in legacy planning deepens connections and ensures your intentions are understood. Involve children in philanthropic activities, teaching them the importance of giving back while nurturing their own sense of purpose. Openly discussing your values and wishes fosters a sense of unity and shared vision, making it easier for your family to carry out your plans. This collaborative approach empowers your loved ones to continue your legacy, preserving the ideals and traditions you hold dear.

Legacy planning extends far beyond the mere allocation of assets. It's about the imprint you leave on the world and the values you pass on to your loved ones. Consider, for instance, the lessons you've learned throughout your life—the triumphs and the trials that have shaped you. These experiences are invaluable, offering wisdom that can guide future generations. By documenting and sharing these life lessons, you provide a road map for your descendants, helping them navigate their own paths with the benefit of your insights. This sharing can take many forms, from written memoirs to recorded interviews, each offering a unique glimpse into your world.

Beyond personal narratives, supporting charitable causes or community projects is a powerful way to create a lasting impact. Establishing scholarships or educational funds can ensure that your commitment to learning and growth continues to benefit others long after you're gone. These initiatives not only support individuals in need but also reflect your values and priorities, serving as a testament to the principles that guided your life. By investing in causes that resonate with you, you contribute to a legacy that transcends time, fostering positive change and community development.

Engaging your family in legacy planning is crucial. Involve your children in philanthropic activities, teaching them the importance of giving back and encouraging them to develop their own sense of social responsibility. This involvement not only strengthens family bonds but also instills values that can be passed down through generations. Open discussions about your values and wishes create an environment of transparency and understanding, ensuring that your legacy is honored in the way you envision. These conversations can be challenging, yet they offer an opportunity for growth and connection, allowing your family to align with your vision and carry it forward.

Consider the story of one family who established a foundation to support local charities, integrating their children into the decision-making process. This approach not only amplified the family's impact but also empowered the younger generation to embrace philanthropy, cultivating a shared commitment to community service. In another instance, an individual chose to preserve their life stories through written memoirs and video recordings.

These personal accounts provided their family with a rich tapestry of memories and insights, fostering a deeper understanding of their roots and the values that defined their family history.

Creating a legacy beyond financial planning is about more than wealth; it's about the enduring influence of your life and ideals. By taking deliberate steps to pass on your values, support meaningful causes, and engage your family, you create a legacy that resonates through time. This legacy serves as a guiding light for your loved ones, offering them the opportunity to build upon the foundation you've laid and continue the work you've begun. These efforts ensure that your presence is felt and celebrated, not just in the assets you leave behind, but in the lives you touch and the world you help shape. As you contemplate your legacy, consider the myriad of ways you can make a difference, leaving a mark that reflects who you are and what you stand for.

Don't move on to the next chapter without doing the following;

1. Ask your lawyer about how to update changes to your plan. Do these changes need to be witnessed or an update on a centralized platform is enough?
2. Do you want to leave something specific to your beneficiaries? Do you want to change your philanthropic cause close to your heart or pass a series of videos to the next generation? Now is the time to make this happen and store them in Dropbox ready to be distributed

Conclusion

Throughout this book, we've explored the intricacies of estate planning, un-raveling the complexities to reveal a clear path forward. From understanding the basics to tailoring strategies to your unique circumstances, we've covered the essential elements of creating a robust and effective plan. We've seen how early and proactive planning can provide peace of mind, ensuring that your wishes are respected and your loved ones are protected.

As a CPA, I've witnessed firsthand the power of estate planning in simplify-ing complex situations. By taking control of your future now, you're giving yourself and your family an invaluable gift—the gift of clarity, security, and peace. Your estate plan is a reflection of your life, your values, and your legacy. It's a testament to the love you have for those closest to you and the impact you wish to make on the world.

Throughout our journey, we've emphasized the importance of customiza-tion. Just as no two lives are identical, no two estate plans should be the same. Your plan should be as unique as your fingerprint, carefully crafted to address your specific needs, goals, and family dynamics. Whether you're a young parent just starting out, a high-net-worth individual with complex assets, or a retiree looking to secure your legacy, your estate plan should be tailored to fit you like a glove.

I've also highlighted the value of getting professional guidance. Estate planning is not a solo endeavor; it's a collaborative process that benefits from the expertise of legal and financial professionals. By building a reliable network of advisors, you can ensure that your plan is legally sound, tax-efficient, and comprehensive. These experts can help you navigate the ever-changing landscape of laws and regulations, keeping your plan up-to-date and effective.

Communication has been another central theme of our discussion. Your estate plan is not a secret to be kept under lock and key; it's a living document that should be shared and discussed with your loved ones. By having open and honest conversations about your intentions, you can avoid misunderstandings, reduce potential conflicts, and ensure that your family is prepared to carry out your wishes. These conversations may not always be easy, but they are essential for creating a shared understanding and a united front.

As we've seen, estate planning is not a one-and-done affair. Life is full of changes, and your plan should evolve with you. By regularly reviewing and updating your plan, you can ensure that it always reflects your current circumstances and preferences. Leveraging digital tools and resources can make this ongoing management more efficient and effective, allowing you to stay on top of your plan with ease.

But estate planning is about more than just distributing assets; it's about creating a legacy that endures. By incorporating philanthropy, passing on values, and sharing life lessons, you can leave a mark that extends far beyond your financial wealth. You have the power to shape the future, to make a difference in the lives of others, and to inspire generations to come.

So, what are the key takeaways from our journey? First, start early. Don't wait for a crisis to begin planning; start now and give yourself the gift of peace of mind. Second, tailor your plan to your unique needs. Cookie-cutter solutions won't cut it; your plan should be as distinctive as you are. Third, seek professional guidance. Surround yourself with a team of experts who can help you navigate the complexities and ensure your plan is rock-solid. Fourth, communicate openly. Share your intentions with your loved ones and foster a culture of transparency and understanding. Finally, remember that your plan is a living document. Regularly review and update it to keep pace with life's changes.

As we conclude this book, I invite you to take the first step in your estate planning journey. Whether that means scheduling a consultation with a professional, organizing your assets, or initiating a conversation with your family, every action brings you closer to securing your legacy. Remember, you're not alone in this process. There's a whole community of individuals on a similar path, ready to offer support, guidance, and shared experiences. Gather the questions that I've suggested at the end of each chapter into a summary to customize your will/trust into something that 100% reflects you and your wishes.

So, go forth with confidence, knowing that you have the power to shape your future and the futures of those you love. Embrace the peace of mind that comes with proactive planning, and enjoy the satisfaction of knowing that your legacy will endure. Your journey to a secure and meaningful future starts now. Let's make it a great one.

References

- *Estate Planning Checklist: A 7-Step Guide* https://www.nerdwallet.com/arti cle/investing/estate-planning/estate-planning
- *Will vs. Trust: Which Is Right For You?* https://www.investopedia.com/articl es/personal-finance/051315/will-vs-trust-difference-between-two.asp
- *How to probate a will: A step-by-step guide* https://www.freewill.com/lear n/how-to-probate-a-will
- *Factors to Consider When Selecting an Executor, Trustee, ...* https://www.essl awfirm.com/articles/factors-to-consider-when-selecting-an-executor- trustee-or-agent-under-a-power-of-lawyer/
- *Estate Planning for Blended Families: Pitfalls and Solutions* https://www.cun ninghamlegal.com/estate-planning-for-blended-families-pitfalls-and- solutions/
- *10 Tips For Choosing A Guardian For Your Minor Child* https://www.forbes.c om/sites/christinefletcher/2020/01/29/10-tips-for-choosing-a-guardia n-for-your-minor-child/
- *Planning for Advanced Asset Protection - Buckley Law* https://buckleylaw.co m/article_posts/planning-for-advanced-asset-protection/
- *The Importance of Cultural Competence in Estate Planning* https://www.acte c.org/resource-center/video/the-importance-of-cultural-competence-i n-estate-planning/#:~:text=Cultural%20competence%20in%20estate% 20planning%20is%20vital%20because%20it%20ensures,with%20the% 20client's%20cultural%20background.
- *10 Estate Planning Myths You Shouldn't Believe* https://www.forbes.com/sit es/financialfinesse/2023/10/02/10-estate-planning-myths-you-should nt-believe/

- *Ways to Avoid Probate* https://www.nolo.com/legal-encyclopedia/ways-avoid-probate
- *10 Common Mistakes in Will Drafting* https://www.jicestates.com/resources/last-will-and-testament/10-common-mistakes-in-will-drafting
- *Estate Taxes: Strategies When Planning Your Estate* https://www.edwardjones.com/us-en/market-news-insights/personal-finance/planning-your-estate/estate-taxes
- *Estate Planning: Listing Your Assets* https://www.universalclass.com/articles/business/estate-planning/estate-planning-listing-your-assets.htm
- *10 Essential Estate Planning Documents* https://thesimonelawfirm.com/estate-planning-documents/
- *Comprehensive Guide to Digital Estate Planning: Secure Your Online Legacy* https://bluenotary.us/digital-estate-planning/#:~:text=Digital%20Estate%20Planning%20Software&text=Companies%20like%20Everplans%2C%20Final%20Security,assets%20
- *Living wills and advance directives for medical decisions* https://www.mayoclinic.org/healthy-lifestyle/consumer-health/in-depth/living-wills/art-20046303#:~:text=By%20planning%20ahead%2C%20you%20can,to%20make%20on%20your%20behalf.
- *When Would I Need To Hire an Estate Planning Lawyer?* https://www.cageandmiles.com/blog/when-would-i-need-to-hire-an-estate-planning-lawyer
- *How Much Does Estate Planning Cost? A Comprehensive Guide* https://www.doaneanddoane.com/how-much-does-estate-planning-cost-a-comprehensive-guide
- *Charitable remainder trusts | Internal Revenue Service* https://www.irs.gov/charities-non-profits/charitable-remainder-trusts
- *The Advantages and Disadvantages of Offshore Trusts* https://www.heritagelawwi.com/the-advantages-and-disadvantages-of-offshore-trusts-what-you-need-to-know
- *International estate planning for Cross-Border Families* https://trustandwill.com/learn/international-estate-planning?srsltid=AfmBOoqYkjyOJ8-74uQd7DwtIPUZNRjtQoZVKGRL_S-4SF-RAox5ohfg

- *What Is an Irrevocable Life Insurance Trust (ILIT)?* https://www.northwester nmutual.com/life-and-money/what-is-an-irrevocable-life-insurance-trust/
- *Case study: Tailored estate planning* https://www.mercer.com/pcs/insights /may-2023/case-study-tailored-estate-planning/
- *Leave a Legacy: Strategies for a Lasting Impact* https://www.usbank.com/w ealth-management/financial-perspectives/trust-and-estate-planning/ what-does-it-mean-to-leave-a-legacy.html#:~:text=Legacy%20planni ng%20involves%20envisioning%20how,advanced%20and%20your%20 legacy%20continues.
- *Estate Planning Strategies for High Net-Worth Individuals* https://www.docr law.com/articles/estate-planning-strategies-for-high-net-worth-indiv iduals
- *Estate Planning for Blended Families: Special Considerations* https://dlfirm.c om/estate-planning-for-blended-families-special-considerations/#:~: text=Equitable%20Asset%20Distribution%3A%20When%20you,ability %20to%20manage%20those%20assets.
- *Life Events That Can Trigger a Change to Your Estate Plan* https://www.bmce stateplanning.com/blog/life-events-change-to-your-estate-plan
- *Year-End Estate Planning Checklist: Reviewing Your Plan* https://www.docrl aw.com/articles/year-end-estate-planning-checklist-reviewing-your-plan
- *Understanding the 2026 Changes to the Estate, Gift, and ...* https://www.husc hblackwell.com/newsandinsights/understanding-the-2026-changes-to-the-estate-gift-and-generation-skipping-tax-exemptions

Also by Emma Maxwell

I'm proud to say this is now my third book. They all complement each other in the personal finance space and are great reads if you liked what you read... .check them out!

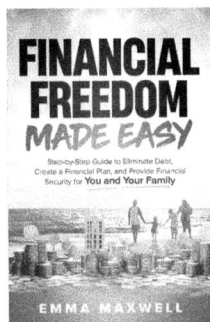

Financial Freedom Made Easy: Step-by-Step Guide to Eliminate Debt, Create a Financial Plan and Provide Security for you and your Family

Achieve Financial Independence and Secure Your Family's Future in Just a Few Simple Steps – Even if You're Starting from Scratch

Financial Freedom Made Easy is your comprehensive, practical guide to financial independence and peace of mind.

Here's just a glimpse of what you'll discover inside:

- **6 practical steps** to create a realistic budget for your family
- The **most effective strategies** for paying off credit card debt, including the *Debt Pay Down* and *Debt Accelerator* methods
- **Emergency Fund 101**: the step-by-step process for building your family's safety net.
- **Investment basics for beginners**: Clear explanations of investing terms and key steps to get you started
- Why **low-risk investment options** can still yield significant returns
- **Easy-to-understand guidelines** for retirement planning to ensure a comfortable future
- **Simple tax planning strategies** to maximize your savings
- How to overcome the **psychological barriers** that hinder good financial habits
- **Real-life success stories** to inspire and motivate your journey

...and so much more!

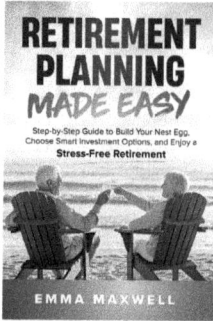

Retirement Planning Made Easy: Step-by-Step Guide to Build Your Nest Egg, Choose Smart Investment Options, and Enjoy a Stress-Free Retirement

With **Retirement Planning Made Easy**, you have a blueprint to navigate your unique financial landscape, tearing down the barriers of complex financial jargon. Inside, you'll learn:

- **How much you will need to afford to retire**, taking into account rising healthcare costs and your future income streams

- Proven strategies to **catch up on savings**, tailored specifically for late starters to ensure that no opportunity is wasted

- **Established investment options** based on your risk profile and age

- **Social Security Made Easy**: How and when to start your Social Security to optimize your retirement

- How to prepare for unpredictable **healthcare costs**, offering options for cover and the costs you may incur in your golden years

- **Estate planning made effortless**: The steps you need to take to secure your legacy and protect your loved ones

- Practical investment adjustments you should make as you approach retirement, preserving your nest egg while maximizing growth potential

- **Debt vs. savings**: A guide to balance priorities effectively and make informed financial decisions to get you debt-free

- How to transition seamlessly to a fulfilling retirement after years in the workforce, **finding new purpose**

- The actionable steps to ensure you **never outlive your savings**, safeguarding your standard of living and independence

- Future-proof strategies for a retirement plan that includes health, lifestyle, and financial aspects

Be sure to check these out on Audible or Amazon

www.ingramcontent.com/pod-product-compliance
Lightning Source LLC
Chambersburg PA
CBHW071435210326

41597CB00020B/3809